MOTIVE TO MURDER

Twenty-one Killing Tales

Motive to Murder

Twenty-one Killing Tales

by
GEORGINA LLOYD

ROBERT HALE · LONDON

© Georgina Lloyd 1988
First published in Great Britain 1988

Robert Hale Limited
Clerkenwell House
Clerkenwell Green
London EC1R 0HT

British Library Cataloguing in Publication Data

Lloyd, Georgina
Motive to murder : twenty-one killing tales.
1. Murder—Case studies
I. Title
364.1'523'0904   HV6513

ISBN 0-7090-3270-6

Photoset in North Wales by
Derek Doyle & Associates, Mold, Clwyd.
Printed in Great Britain by
St Edmundsbury Press Ltd, Bury St Edmunds, Suffolk.
Bound by WBC Bookbinders Limited.

Contents

Introduction

I have chosen the cases for this book to provide examples from a very wide spectrum of motives for murder.

What makes a person kill?

The motives for murder are many and varied, but they can be roughly divided into four main categories: premeditated murder for gain, such as George Joseph Smith ('Brides in the Bath'), or Nurse Dorothea Waddingham, who poisoned two elderly patients in her private nursing home after tricking them into making a will in her favour. The second category consists of those who kill from jealousy or anger, such as the man who kills his wife and/or her lover, whether premeditated or on an impulse.

The third main category includes the man who hits his wife during a quarrel and unwittingly strikes her in a vulnerable spot, killing her, or maybe squeezes her and unwittingly cuts off her breathing. One or two cases come to mind in which a man shook his wife and she spun round in an effort to escape, striking her head on the edge of a door or fender or some such object, with fatal results. These cases are, perhaps, not murder *sensu strictu*, since the victim's death was never intended. However, I have included them in this third category simply because violence was used which led to the death of the victim. Although, of course, this is technically manslaughter, one must not lose sight of the fact that if the violent assault had not occurred in the first place, death would not have ensued.

I should perhaps here also include rapists who squeeze the throats of their victims or clap a hand over their mouths simply to stifle their screams or to stop them from crying out – in other words, to enable the perpetrator to pursue his aim and escape detection. No homicidal impulse is present, and the death of the victim was never intended: 'I didn't mean to kill her – I did it just to shut her up', as one such man said. Legally this, too, is manslaughter. It is all too easy to stop someone breathing by pressing the throat, and when a hand – especially a large male hand – is clamped over a victim's mouth, it often lands over the nose as well, thus effectively obstructing all the air passages. The first the rapist knows about what he has unintentionally brought about is when the victim suddenly goes limp and slumps unconscious. Usually the perpetrator will flee in panic, thinking that he has killed her – which, of course, can occur in one of two ways: either she is already dead when he leaves her, or she dies subsequently because resuscitation procedures were not applied immediately.

The fourth main category consists of mentally sick persons, suffering from psychopathic or psychotic disorders of the mind, with a compulsion to kill, often sexually motivated. Even those who aver that they had no sexual motive – such as a man who says he kills prostitutes 'to cleanse the streets' – still almost invariably has a *subconscious* sexual motive, even though he may not be consciously aware of it.

Psychopaths and psychotics fall into various categories, such as paranoiacs, schizophrenics, manic-depressives and other lesser-known types. All these are not merely the labels of medical terminology but are well-defined syndromes. In layman's terms, some killers have persecution mania and wish to destroy those who they feel to be their enemies; others have a deep-seated compulsion to destroy those who reflect the image of someone they hate, such as a repressive mother or a frigid wife, or a girlfriend who has jilted them for another man.

Yet others feel subconsciously that sex is dirty or sinful – often as a result of indoctrination along these lines by their parents after they had reached puberty. They are therefore unable to reconcile these feelings with their own normal sexual impulses and are unable to marry or enter into a meaningful relationship with a girl. Consequently they will rape a woman and then kill her afterwards in an effort to blot out the cause of their own downfall and shame.

Sometimes a mentally sick murderer will, after the killing, enter a state known as a mental 'fugue', during which his consciousness blots out all memory of his crime. This type of amnesia is his subconscious mind's defence reaction to enable him to live with himself. In fact these murderers are among the most difficult to detect because, between murders, they act perfectly normally and even their close family and friends would never suspect them. 'He's the very last person who would kill anybody!' the father of one such man said. 'Why, he registered as a conscientious objector to avoid the draft – he was terrified of being ordered to kill out there in 'Nam. He wouldn't hurt a fly.' This particular young man raped and killed fourteen young girls ....

There is, perhaps, little we can do with sane men who kill except award them prison sentences of varying lengths appropriate to their offences. But the fourth category – the homicidal psychopaths and psychotics – are sick men, just as a man with a physical disease is sick: the only difference is that his sickness is a disorder or disease of the mind. Although I would be the first to admit that the killer must be kept in custody for the safety of the public, prison is not the answer.

My researches have indicated that very many of such murderers who were sent to prison asked – even begged – for medical treatment. They were refused on various grounds – the cost, the non-availability of suitable medical personnel and so on. Clearly what is required are more secure hospitals, not prisons.

The cold-blooded killer who murders for gain should, rightly, be sentenced to a term of imprisonment, but the psychopath and the psychotic should receive appropriate treatment in a secure psychiatric hospital. Murder is never a solution to a problem or situation, and neither is the hopelessness of life in prison for the murderer who has killed as a direct result of the processes of a deranged mind.

We all have responsibilities towards our fellow men and women; we are all our brother's keeper in one sense or another. But while abhorring crime and brutality, we should respect all humanity. If, understandably, we sometimes find it difficult to respect the humanity of a person guilty of a horrendous and ghastly murder, or murders, we can at least make an effort to understand the underlying motive, and act on the light of that knowledge.

Georgina Lloyd
1987

1

The Kiss of Death

The village of Czinkota is but a few miles from Budapest, the capital of Hungary, as the crow flies. In the days of World War I it was little more than a hamlet, and a sleepy one at that. Its inhabitants were stolid men and women of peasant stock, who tilled the soil, often from the first light of dawn until it became too dark to see. They used antiquated ploughs drawn by oxen and irrigated their fields with water drawn from adjacent wells and hauled in buckets. A few of the village men pursued trades and crafts such as those of the village carpenter, blacksmith, farrier, cooper or tinsmith.

The motor car was a fairly recent innovation at that time, but even the more affluent of the farmers could not use their cars even if they had them, because of the wartime embargo on the use of petrol for civilian purposes. Vast quantities of fuel were required to feed into the ever-open maw of the military machine. It was inevitable, therefore, that a black market for petrol operated in Czinkota as elsewhere. The black market was not just the monopoly of sophisticated city-slickers.

Police were sent from Budapest to ferret out the secret petrol-hoarders in all the rural areas, and when they came to Czinkota they called first at the village inn. The innkeeper, they surmised, would know everybody – or nearly everybody – and might have a very good idea as to who were likely suspects for the illegal hoarding and selling of petrol. The innkeeper, intimidated by four burly policemen who made it abundantly clear that they would not be fobbed off with excuses, began to sing like a canary. The tinsmith, he blabbed in fear-ridden tones, might be worth a visit. The tinsmith who lived on the hill. Only thing was, he said, he was not actually in residence as he had been called up for his military service in the spring of 1914. But his house – ah, that was different. Before he had left to join the army he had padlocked all the doors and set steel bars into all the windows. It was now a veritable fortress. Now why should a humble tinsmith leave his house with such security? Could it be that he had something to hide? Like, for example, supplies of illegal petrol? The innkeeper's voice dropped to a conspiratorial whisper. The tinsmith, he said, was known to have sold black market petrol from time to time – very much *sub rosa*, of course.

The police now dropped their browbeating approach and stood the loose-tongued innkeeper a tankard of ale for his trouble. Then they made their way up the hill to the two-storey wooden house with its smithy alongside. The date of their visit was 7 May 1916.

One of the policemen forced a door with a crowbar, and the four officers entered the house. They went systematically through the living-rooms and bedrooms, but found nothing suspicious to arouse their interest. All that remained now was to search the attic, and they climbed the rickety ladder which swung precariously from two large iron hooks in the edge of the trapdoor. No sooner had the first officer entered the attic than a triumphant cry went up. 'The innkeeper was right! There's petrol here all right – come and see for yourselves. *Seven hundred-gallon casks!*'

The policemen stared in frank disbelief. How could the tinsmith have amassed such a vast quantity of petrol? It must be worth a fortune on the black market. No wonder he wasn't very keen to go into the army, one of them remembered. Army pay wouldn't keep him in shirt buttons.

The seven casks were supported on trestles and lined up against the far wall. How on earth the tinsmith could possibly have hauled them up the ladder was a puzzle. No doubt he had fixed up some kind of block and tackle arrangement, roped each cask and hauled it up in that way.

The four policemen dragged one of the casks off its supporting trestle and hauled it into the middle of the floor. It had been hermetically sealed as only a tinsmith knew how. It was decided to open the cask, and with a good deal of difficulty the men managed to prise it open with the aid of a hatchet, a pickaxe and a saw. When at last, sweating from the effort, they managed to lift the heavy lid, their triumph turned quickly to disappointment. The odour that hit their nostrils was not the acrid smell of petrol. It was not even wine, or stronger liquor. It was the stench of decay – the decomposition of human flesh. A few old clothes were bundled on top of the contents, which were revealed in all their horror as the policemen pulled out the rotting rags that had once been female garments. Beneath lay the naked body of a woman, coiled to fit into the confined space of the barrel. The limbs had been trussed up to the torso like a chicken, and the corpse, which was well-preserved, bore the unmistakable mark of the strangler's noose.

Reinforcements, including a senior officer, were sent from Budapest, and using stronger gear than the makeshift implements with which the first cask had been opened, all seven kegs were soon opened to reveal their grisly contents. Each barrel contained a dead woman; all were naked with their clothes piled on top of them. All had been strangled. None was immediately identifiable, although all were well-preserved in their hermetically-sealed coffins. The medical examiner subsequently proved that the victims had been stored in the tinsmith's attic for at least two years. This tallied with the time at which he had left the village to join the army, shortly after the outbreak of hostilities in 1914.

Eventually all seven victims were identified. One was the daughter of the innkeeper who had given the police the tip-off about the supposed 'petrol hoard' at the tinsmith's house. She had gone missing in November 1913, but it had been thought that she had left to look for a job in Budapest, being bored with the quiet and uneventful life of Czinkota. Another young girl was also a former resident of the village. Four of the women, all young, were from Budapest, and the seventh victim was an Austrian girl from Vienna.

The police, finding no further bodies in the house, decided to dig up the garden, where they soon found a further ten victims, all young women, buried in shallow graves. More were found in a nearby wood. All these buried victims, the medical examiner reported, had been killed before the women in the casks had met their end. It would seem, the police said, that the tinsmith had run out of space in his garden, and had then resorted to burying the cadavers in the wood, but had probably found this too risky to continue. He had then pressed into service his skills as a tinsmith to seal the seven victims in the kegs in such a way as to ensure that there would be no leakage of tell-tale odours or body fluids. And the murders might have gone undiscovered had it not been for the wartime shortage of petrol and a talkative innkeeper ....

It was now time for the police to turn their attention to the absent tinsmith himself and investigate his activities before his call to the colours. His name was Bela Kiss, and it seems that before he left Czinkota he had been very active indeed. A search of the bureau in his house had provided unassailable proof. More than a hundred pawn tickets were found, relating to such items as jewellery, fur coats and better-class female clothing and shoes, suitcases and portmanteaus and other valuables. There were dozens of letters, and copies of advertisements which he had placed in various newspapers in Hungary and Austria. Using the name Hoffmann, he had posed as a landed gentleman seeking matrimony, or in some cases offering employment. He also posed as a matrimonial agent who could put suitable young ladies 'of good character and sound financial position' in touch with gentlemen of similar assets for the purpose of matrimony. Letters from women found in the bureau described their monetary assets in glowing terms; these letters had been marked with a tick. Others, seemingly poor but honest, had been crossed through. Several dozen copies of Bela Kiss's portrait were also found, ready to send to future victims, no doubt, had not war intervened.

The photographs enabled the police to make extensive inquiries about his pre-war activities. Several high-class restaurants in Budapest knew him as a regular customer, and it had frequently been observed that he was invariably accompanied by a different female companion, usually young and good-looking and who usually paid the bill.

It was a much more difficult task to find Bela Kiss. The War Office confirmed his name and army number and the regiment in which he had enlisted. However, the records showed that he had apparently died of fever while serving in Serbia. The police did not simply take the War Office's word for it – they sent two officers out to the field hospital in Serbia to check the records personally. The death of Bela Kiss, private soldier, had been entered, giving his correct date of birth – 6 April 1881 – and describing his height as 1m 73cm (5ft. 8in.). This made one of the police officers suspicious, since he had definite knowledge that Kiss had been 1m 80cm (5ft. 11in.) tall.

The officer questioned nurses at the hospital, and his suspicions were reinforced when one of the nurses told him that 'the patient had been such a nice lad and much too young to die' and that he had 'fair hair and blue eyes'. Kiss had been thirty-five with a swarthy complexion and black hair. The 'nice lad' had been only eighteen ....

Further investigation by the two officers revealed that Kiss had indeed been wounded in the war and transferred to that military hospital, and had used his admission to exchange identity discs with another more seriously-wounded soldier who later died. Soon afterwards he left the hospital and deserted the army, and in 1919 reports were received by the police that he had been spotted in Budapest city centre. However, despite intensive searching, the police were unable to find him.

For the next five years there were no alleged sightings of the homicidal tinsmith, until late in 1924 a story persisted that he had joined the French Foreign Legion in the name of Hoffmann and deserted shortly thereafter. Then, in 1932, an American detective believed that he had seen him in New York City. He was so convinced of his elusive quarry's identity that he spent more than two years trying to locate him. But all his efforts proved fruitless.

To this day, no one knows for certain what happened to the tinsmith of Czinkota who had sealed his victims in casks with the Kiss of death, and to whom a total of twenty-four murders are attributed.

2

The Sausage-maker of Chicago

Few murders have ever shocked the citizens of Chicago, Illinois, so much as the gruesome killing of Louisa Luetgert in 1897 by her husband Adolf, one of the leading butchers in the city at that time. He had emigrated from his native Germany in the 1870s and within three years he had earned the reputation of making the best German sausages in the city, and possibly in the state. Customers flocked to buy his products – not only the sizeable immigrant German population of the city but also other citizens of various nationalities and ethnic origins who enjoyed good, substantial food – the Dutch, the Poles, and many others who made up the motley population of Chicago.

It seems that Adolf Luetgert himself, too, enjoyed good and substantial fare – too much for his own good. He tipped the scales at a hefty 250 pounds, or close eighteen stone. His girth could rival that of the beer belly of even the most dedicated of the drinkers who patronized Chicago's taverns – and doubtless beer, too, contributed not a little to his own. Good German beer, at that.

Even his gastronomic appetites, however, came but a poor second to his tremendous sexual ones. He had no fewer than three regular mistresses as well as his wife, and it was common knowledge that in a small office at his works he had a bed installed for his use in company with his typists, secretaries and factory workwomen. This, it was said, was the reason why 'The Boss' could very rarely be found available at his works by the various salesmen, representatives and other callers who arrived there to see him about their legitimate business.

Adolf Luetgert was happy and contented with this set-up, except for one thing: his wife was a nagging shrew. 'She annoys me,' he told one mistress. 'I could take her and crush her!' he is on record as having said to another. 'She is as cold as a dead fish!' he is reported to have told a secretary. And yet another office worker is reputed to have said that Adolf Luetgert told her, during the course of his dalliance with her, that sex with his wife was 'like trying to flog a dead horse'.

One evening Louisa Luetgert had arranged to visit her mother. It was in late April 1897. There was little love lost between Adolf Luetgert and his mother-in-law, but he was pleased to allow Louisa to go and visit her mother whenever she liked. The longer she stayed the better, for Adolf could then have some temporary respite from his wife's caustic tongue. So when she did not return, and people asked him where she was, he naturally replied that she was staying at her mother's. He appeared considerably shocked, therefore, when his mother-in-law herself visited him at his works demanding to know what had happened to her daughter.

'I understood she was staying with you,' he replied. 'She told me she was going out to visit you, and when she did not come back I naturally assumed she was staying at your house, although she had not told me that she intended to do so on that occasion.'

'She has not visited me at all,' the woman replied.

'Then where can she be?' said Adolf.

'I'm asking you,' said the mother-in-law. 'You know it's not like her to go anywhere for any length of time without telling either you or me where she is going and how long she will be away. I think we should report her missing to the police. Something must have happened to her.'

'Oh, no!' answered Adolf. 'As a prominent businessman in this city, I could not possibly afford a scandal. My business would be ruined!'

'Why – do you think she's run off with another man?' demanded his mother-in-law.

'I shouldn't think so – but you never know with women,' Adolf replied. 'Tell you what I'll do – I'll hire private detectives to find her. They're very good, you know. Nine times out of ten they find the person they're looking for.'

The mother of Louisa Luetgert had to be content with this for the time being, but after a few days had passed and there was still no news of the missing woman, her mother held a conference at her home with several relatives, without informing Adolf, and they decided that the police should be informed. Several relatives who knew Louisa well voiced the opinion that she was not the kind of woman who would run off with another man, and those of the relatives who knew her husband averred that he was not the type of man who would spend money on hiring private detectives, but rather would be secretly pleased that she had gone off somewhere – perhaps back to Germany – so that he could enjoy some peace and quiet. Her scolding propensities were well known. Accordingly, on 1 May 1897 the relatives went to the police and reported Louisa Luetgert missing.

When a wife is missing, the husband is always the first suspect. The police gave Adolf a hard time, interrogating him at length. He stuck to his story that she had gone out, saying she was going to visit her mother, and had not come back, and that he had no idea where she had gone, since her mother had not seen her. Nothing the police said would make him budge. He did admit that he had never actually hired any private detectives, although, he said, he had intended to do so. He gave the police the distinct impression that he was far more concerned about the effect of a scandal on his business, than about the whereabouts of his wife.

The police could see that they were getting absolutely nowhere by merely questioning the master butcher. They decided to search his entire factory from top to bottom. Asked what the bed in the small office was for, Adolf replied that it was for him to sleep in when he had to work late and it was hardly worth going home in the early hours when he had to be back by 7 a.m. at the works. The detectives nodded, but said little. Rumours had already reached them of its true purpose – in fact the rumours had been in circulation for quite some time. Adolf Luetgert was already notorious as a Lothario.

Finally, the police decided to empty the steam vats, one after another, and search the sludge at the bottom. The first three vats produced nothing suspicious, but the fourth one confirmed the suspicions which they had held all along but had not communicated to their suspect. In the sludge at the bottom of the vat they found human bone fragments, human teeth, and two gold wedding rings, one of which was engraved with the initials L.L. Louisa Luetgert's mother and several other relatives all identified both rings as having belonged to the missing woman.

Adolf Luetgert was taken into custody and charged with the murder of his wife. He strongly denied the charge, insisting that he knew nothing of her whereabouts. He denied that the bone fragments could be human, pointing out that pig meat was used in the manufacture of his sausages and that anatomically pig bones, to the layman, bore some resemblance to human bones. The teeth, he said, could be false teeth which one of his factory workers had let fall into the vat during cleaning operations. The rings were certainly not his wife's, he averred; his wife suffered from swollen, arthritic finger joints and had been unable to remove either of her rings for years. 'Ask her mother!' he told police interrogators. 'She will be able to tell you!'

The police did just that, and Louisa Luetgert's mother confirmed that both the rings were her daughter's property. Confronted with this statement, Luetgert tried to bluff things out. 'I should know – I'm her husband!' he stormed. 'They are not my wife's rings. My wife's mother is over seventy and short-sighted. Surely you do not believe her word against mine?' The police pointed out that one ring bore his wife's initials. 'Don't be stupid!' Luetgert ranted. 'My wife is not the only woman with the initials L.L. There must be hundreds – maybe even thousands – of women with the same initials in Chicago!' To which the interrogator felt bound to reply that that might indeed be so, but that it was most unlikely that one of these women would have come and dropped her ring into Adolf's steam vat.

By now the forensic pathologist had examined the bone fragments which had been discovered in the sludge at the bottom of the vat, and pronounced them as definitely human. He had also examined the teeth, and Louisa Luetgert's dentist, Herr Hans Kaufman, was asked to check them with his records. He positively identified them as teeth which he had supplied to Louisa Luetgert as part of a false denture plate in 1892.

Police stated that it was known that Louisa Luetgert could not have removed her rings herself, so she had been literally melted out of them. In fact, Adolf had melted his unfortunate wife's entire body in Vat No. 4 at his meat plant and made her part of his sausage production line. Police could, however, only conjecture how he had killed her, as no weapon was ever found; they surmised that the most likely method was that he had stabbed her to death with one of the sharp knives used in the butchery department. How he had lured her into the steam vat department was also a mystery, but for a man with as persuasive a line of chat as Adolf, it was probably quite easy.

The trial of Adolf Luetgert was sensational. Nothing like it had ever before been known in Chicago. The trial lasted several days, and every day hordes of people thronged the streets outside the court, which was crowded to capacity; there was, after all, a limit to the number of people the public gallery could hold. One mistress after another took the stand to testify against him, followed by a long procession of typists, secretaries and factory women who had been gullible enough to fall for the plausible blandishments of the tubby Don Juan, who looked more like a professional wrestler than a master butcher. Despite the incontrovertible evidence against him, Luetgert denied all knowledge of the crime to the end, and maintained his innocence of any knowledge of what had happened to his wife. He was visibly shocked, however, at seeing so many of his erstwhile bedfellows turn against him and denounce him on the stand.

All his protestations, however, availed him nothing, and he was convicted of murder in the first degree. He was sentenced to life imprisonment, and died in Joliet Prison in 1911, where the only bed he knew for fourteen years was a narrow wooden pallet in his cell. He never saw another woman for the rest of his life – not even his mother-in-law.

Adolf Luetgert was, however, well-remembered for many years after his death. Sales of sausage-meat were damaged for a very long time in Chicago, and German sausages in particular were boycotted by the nauseated population. Luetgert's factory was closed, and those Germans who were particularly fond of their national specialities would take a trip out of Chicago and buy them in another town, or even over the border in Michigan.

Even thirty years later, according to one report published in a magazine in 1941, children playing in the streets of Chicago could still be heard chanting:

> Adolf was a dirty rat
> Who boiled his wife for sausage fat

And it wasn't Adolf Hitler they were referring to ....

3

A Head by Candlelight

It had been nine days since Patrick O'Leary, a forty-year-old farmer of Kilkerrin, Co. Cork, had been seen around the village. He lived with his elderly widowed mother, Mrs Hannah O'Leary, his sisters, one also named Hannah and the other Mary Anne, and his brother Cornelius, known as Con. Their father, Patrick O'Leary, had died three years earlier, leaving his small farm to his widow for life and after her death to Patrick, the eldest son, who was charged with the payment of £350 to Mary Anne and a right of residence to Hannah and Con for life. This was a common arrangement among Irish smallholders. The property was worth about £1,100, which was a considerable sum for a smallholder in the rural Ireland of the 1920s.

Patrick had last been seen on 26 February 1925, when a friend passing by saw him going into the hayloft behind the house at about 9.30 p.m. – presumably on his way to bed, for he habitually slept in the hayloft.

The days passed and no one saw Patrick about as they usually did, and, as usual in such a small community, tongues (mainly female) began to wag. One neighbour, inquiring of Con where his brother was, asked him whether he did not think his disappearance should be reported to the Gardaí. 'Of course not!' Con replied. 'There is no need. He'll be back any day.' The story given out by the O'Learys was that Patrick had gone to Bandon Fair, a few miles away, at three o'clock on 27 February, to sell a horse, and that as he frequently stayed away from home for several days at a time his absence caused them no concern.

On 7 March Frank Walsh, a ten-year-old boy from the village, was crossing one of the O'Learys' fields and found a potato sack lying under a furze bush. With the curiosity of all small boys he opened it. After one look inside, he dropped it hastily and ran screaming home to tell his mother of his find. Mrs Walsh immediately called the Gardaí, two of whom were despatched to the farm and examined the contents of the sack, in which they found a human head, crudely hacked from the body. They knew everyone in the village.

'It's Pat!' cried one.

'That is indeed Pat!' agreed the other.

The sack containing the head was only the first of the grisly finds to come. In another sack in an adjoining field was a human arm severed at the shoulder and still wearing a shirt sleeve. After reporting their first find, the Gardaí were detailed to search the rest of the farm, and the horror was multiplied with each fresh discovery of dismembered human remains in places of greater or lesser concealment, until the final obscenity, when the O'Learys' dog trotted out of a wood with a human arm between its jaws, still clad in a bloody shirt sleeve. When all the parts had been collected, including the torso, the body was still incomplete. The missing parts were never found.

The first thing the Gardaí did after their grim discoveries was to call upon the O'Learys. Con opened the door. When the Gardaí asked him where his brother was he told them the story about going to Bandon to sell a horse and staying there a few days. Asked why he had not reported him as missing after such a long absence, Con replied that he did not think it was necessary.

'Nine days is a long time for him to be away,' persisted the Gardaí.

'It was a habit of his to go away like that,' was the calm rejoinder. 'We expect him to return any day.'

This was a blatant lie, as the sergeant found out very soon; in fact several neighbours averred that Patrick had never been known to stay away in this fashion.

Con was then asked to go to the field where the head had been found, accompanied by Sgt. Devoy. Sgt. Reynolds was already there keeping guard over the remains. Con, shown the head and asked whether it was his brother's, studied it for a few moments, and then said, 'Yes, that is Pat.' He appeared totally unmoved by the experience.

The face had been considerably disfigured by violence, and it could conceivably have been less than easy to identify, but Sgt. Devoy, who had known Patrick O'Leary since he was a boy, had no difficulty at all in recognizing the head, so he thought it strange, to say the least, that the man's own brother had hesitated. Later at least three neighbours identified his head without hesitation.

Just then Supt. Troy arrived on the scene and asked Con whether the head was Pat's. Surprisingly, Con replied, 'I do not know whose head it is.'

'But haven't you just identified it to me?' exclaimed Sgt. Devoy.

'I did,' replied Con, but gave no explanation for this sudden *volte face*, and was not asked to provide one. At the inquest Con said that when he had been asked by Supt. Troy to identify the head he was in doubt, although he had not felt any doubt when Sgt. Devoy had asked him.

The remains were taken to the village and laid on a table in a small room behind a public house. Con was taken there, accompanied by Supt. Troy; Mary Anne and Hannah had also been brought along. Supt. Troy interviewed Hannah first. She told him the same Bandon story, and he asked her at what time Patrick had left.

'Three o'clock,' she replied.

Asked whether her brother Con was on speaking terms with Patrick, she replied, 'Yes – why shouldn't he be?'

Troy then asked her whether Patrick had any enemies.

'Our Pat had no enemies.'

Asked whether Patrick had ever left home before, Hannah's answer flatly contradicted Con's earlier reply to the same question.

'No, he never did.'

'Would you be surprised if I told you that he was dead?' continued Troy.

'I would not believe you,' the woman replied. 'Why should he be dead? He was a strong man and could defend himself as well as anybody.'

'Would you be surprised if I told you that he has been murdered?'

'I would not believe you. Who would want to murder him?'

Having completed his questioning, the superintendent took Hannah into the small room, leaving Mary Anne and Con outside. The room was lighted with flickering candles, which threw weird shadows across the table on which the dead man's remains were displayed. When the two entered, Sgt. Devoy and Sgt. Reynolds were already there with a Dr Murphy. The head was shown to Hannah and Troy asked her whether she could identify it. She said nothing, and did not even flinch, but looked at it for several moments, then looked away and glanced around the room. Asked the same question again, she said, simply, 'No.'

The head was then moved so that Hannah could see it full face on. She turned her eyes upon it. Nobody spoke, but the watchers gazed with horror upon this unnatural sister as she stood there, quite unmoved by the ghastly sight. Then she spoke. 'Pat was not so thin on top,' she observed. 'This one is bald.'

Troy then sent her out of the room, and called in Mary Anne, who had no difficulty at all in recognizing her brother's head. Troy then called Hannah back. When Hannah entered, Troy asked Mary Anne whose head it was.

'Pat's,' she said without a moment's hesitation.

Then Troy turned to Hannah again. 'Take a better look,' he said.

She did so, and after a short silence she said, 'It is not Pat's head.'

Troy asked her once more, and she took a longer look at the head. As Troy later recounted at the trial, she now began to display some interest in it, and after a while she said, 'I am beginning to think that it might be him.' Then, after a further interval, she agreed. 'Yes, it is Pat, sure enough.' Inevitably one is led to wonder what Hannah thought she was achieving by this unconvincing performance.

Troy, having secured two identifications, wanted a third, and summoned Con. In his presence the two women repeated that the head was their brother's, but Con disagreed, saying that he was not sure that it was even like Pat's. He looked at the head from different angles, had it turned round, hesitated again, and then, asked once more by Supt. Troy, he said that it was. The dreadful scene was now at an end.

The inquest was held the following day, and the first witness called by Supt. Troy, representing the Gardaí, was Con O'Leary. The coroner asked him whether he wanted to give evidence, pointing out that he was not required to do so but that if he did it would be taken down in writing and that if he were later charged with any crime in connection with the death of his brother what he said could be given in evidence at his trial. Con replied that he wished to give evidence, and gave a deposition most of which could not have been true, although it did not directly implicate him in the murder. His deposition was as follows.

'I last saw my brother alive on Monday night 25 February at about half-nine or ten o'clock. I was just going into the house as he was going out. I saw him open the loft door, go in and close the door after him. The following Tuesday morning 26 February I heard my brother knocking about in the house, but I did not see him. My sister Hannah told me that she had seen him.' His deposition continued that Hannah had told him that Patrick had come in for breakfast early as he was going to Bandon Fair between three and four o'clock. She said that he had his breakfast in the kitchen. She would have had to light the fire in order to prepare it. 'I am a heavy sleeper', the deposition continued, 'and although I was in the room next to the kitchen I did not hear Patrick come in or go out. I have no idea what my brother's business was at Bandon Fair except that my sister Hannah had said that he was going to sell a horse ... I thought this rather odd, as the horse was still in the stable later the same day and was still there on Wednesday morning, and I have been feeding it since last Friday ... The chopped furze which was fed to the horses was stored in the loft where my brother used to sleep. Somebody used to go into the loft every day to fetch the food for the horses. Potatoes were also stored there. Potatoes are kept nowhere else on the farm and are required in the kitchen every day. I was in the loft at least once every day since my brother left to fetch horse feed and potatoes. I am not sure whether my brother's bed had been slept in after the night of the Monday before he was going to the Fair. I never took any notice of the bed ... I did not look for my brother since 27 February, nor did I ask any people whether they had seen him, as I thought he would turn up any day. My mother and sisters were also wondering why Patrick had not returned sooner, and they discussed it with me. I said I thought he might possibly have found some work somewhere, in Cork, maybe, or somewhere else, and would come back at the end of the job.'

The funeral took place from the O'Leary home on the day

after the inquest. The remains had been removed to the house and were on view at the wake in accordance with rural Irish custom of the times. This particular instance of the custom had a most ghoulish atmosphere, the open coffin displaying the incomplete dismembered body of the deceased. The neighbours had gathered, and the four O'Learys were dispensing the customary hospitality. What shocked the neighbours profoundly was that the O'Learys were showing no great concern, much less grief. All those who had been for days aghast and incredulous at the manner of Patrick O'Leary's death were now horrified at the apparent callousness of the family. One neighbour, William Whelton, went so far as to remonstrate with Con, pointing out that 'suspicion' (though he did not specify whose) was strongly against him, and that it was up to him to find the perpetrator of the outrage and bring him to justice, thus clearing the cloud which hung over his head. Con continued to protest his innocence, while the other three members of the family kept silent.

Later the same evening another guest, a Mrs McCarthy, addressed remarks in a similar vein to the old lady, adding, 'It's a great shame, Mrs O'Leary, to see your son in such a situation.' The *materfamilias* did not reply, nor did either of her daughters, and Con repeated once more his earlier words: 'I am innocent.' All were shocked by the silence of the O'Leary women. Tittle-tattle was running rife in the village. Suspicion, of course, is not proof, but many of the villagers were not averse to voicing their own theories as to who had murdered Patrick O'Leary ....

The Gardaí's continued investigations showed beyond any doubt that the murder had been committed while Patrick was in bed asleep, and must have been committed by one of the family. But which one? Whoever actually struck the fatal blows had either pre-arranged it with the others, or involved them afterwards in the disposal of the body. In the latter event they would have been guilty of being accessories after the fact, which carried the penalty of life imprisonment; but the most likely theory was a conspiracy to murder. The Gardaí, however, did not attempt to solve these legal problems; they dealt with the matter by arresting all four, on 14 March, one week after the head had been found. All were charged with murder and conspiracy to murder. When Con was charged he did not reply. When Hannah was charged she replied, 'I had nothing to do with it.' Mary Anne's answer to the charge was 'I was not there at all that night. Ask the woman whose house I slept in.' Mrs O'Leary said that she knew nothing about any plot, and was innocent. This was probably true; she was seventy-five.

While the trial was pending, Mary Anne died from cancer in prison. Since the prosecution had no case against Mrs O'Leary, they entered a plea of *nolle prosequi* on her behalf (which meant that there was no case to record or pursue), and she was released. The trial now proceeded against Con and Hannah only, who were not charged with conspiracy but with murder, and, as Mr Carrigan, KC, told the jury in his opening speech, it was obviously a case of concerted murder, meaning that the two defendants together had acted equally as principals in the commission of the crime. Mary Anne being dead, nothing was said about her part in it, whatever that might have been, nor did Mr Carrigan attempt to show which of the pair had delivered the fatal blows. He could not, nor could anyone else except the two who were in the dock, and they were not called to give evidence.

The proof of the crime and the manner of its commission presented no problems for the prosecution. The headboard of Patrick O'Leary's bed showed evidence of having been wiped, but wormholes in the wood were still filled with dried blood. The bed-frame and the floor beneath were bloodstained, and the inside of the loft roof showed blood from arterial spurting. The bedclothes were free of stains, and the bolster, pillow, quilt and blankets which were on the bed when the Gardaí came to search the farm looked fresh, as though the bed had not been in use for some time. These had probably been substituted for the ones that had been in use when Patrick was killed; indeed, it is difficult to see how blood could be found on the bed-frame and yet the bedclothes escape. The mattress itself was missing, but pieces of a bloodstained mattress were found in a field near the house. These matched fragments of a mattress imperfectly hidden in the loft. It is amazing how careless the murderer, or murderers, were in their attempts to dispose of incriminating evidence; the Gardaí had no trouble at all in finding it.

Supt. Troy related to the court how, after he had completed

his search of the house and loft, he had turned his attention to the overgrown garden. Under six-foot-high weeds, Troy found a pair of trousers which Con had agreed were his brother's best trousers, although Patrick was supposed to have worn them to go to the Fair. Garda McHugh, who was searching in the adjoining field, had appeared shortly afterwards with a jacket which matched the trousers and which he had found in a ditch. Con obligingly confirmed that this, too, was Patrick's jacket. Soon after finding the jacket, McHugh had discovered a severed human leg concealed under some furze. When shown the leg Con had made no reply.

The medical evidence was that the dismemberment was probably effected by a blunt, non-surgical instrument; the jagged and rough edges of the cuts could have been made by a hatchet or a billhook. The head of the unfortunate victim had been severely injured, the right side of the face having been partially pulped with extreme violence. The base of the skull, the left cheekbone and the nose were all extensively fractured. The head wounds were circular, and could have been inflicted with a hammer or with the blunt end of a hatchet.

Cross-examined by Mr Joseph A. McCarthy, defending, the pathologist agreed that a good-sized stone could have caused the wounds, and that both the head injuries and the dismemberment could have been the work of one person. The cause of death was the skull fracture. The first blow had probably been the one on the right side of the head which, if inflicted during sleep, would have immediately stunned the victim. The pathologist thought it very unlikely that the murderer, or murderers, tackled their victim while he was awake. A juror's question supported this view. Were there any defensive wounds on arms or hands that would indicate a struggle? The answer was no.

One of the most striking features of the behaviour of the four O'Learys was their silence about Patrick's disappearance – 'the silence of death', as Mr Justice Hanna, the trial judge, called it. To no single person did any one of the four volunteer the information that Patrick had gone away and not returned; only when asked did any of them give the story of his supposed trip to Bandon Fair. One neighbour, a Miss Bridget O'Regan, who lived across the road from the

O'Learys, said in evidence that she had not realized that Patrick was missing until she heard some gossip in the village. On the day after the finding of the head she and her brother met Con O'Leary walking along the road, and her brother asked him, 'Con, is that Paddy in the bag?'

'Yes,' was the reply.

'It's a bad case, then?' said Miss O'Regan.

'It's awful,' replied Con, and, after another of his oft-echoed remarks about his innocence, he then added a most curious observation: 'The man that did the like of it did it before.'

This would appear to have been an attempt to lay the blame for the crime on a mythical stranger – a psychopath, perhaps.

On their counsel's advice neither of the two had gone into the witness-box, nor did they exercise their right to make an unsworn statement of evidence from the dock, on which they could not have been cross-examined.

The prosecution in a criminal trial is prohibited by law from commenting on the failure of accused persons to give evidence, but the judge is not, and Mr Justice Hanna, in his charge to the jury, spoke unfavourably of their refusal and of their failure to explain things that required clarification. He also remarked upon the striking similarity of the behaviour of Con and Hannah O'Leary, the same false stories told by both, the almost identical conduct of the two when confronted with the head, and their callous indifference when the remains were found and on the night of the wake.

The jury retired for only half an hour before finding both the accused guilty, but the foreman announced that the majority of the jury wished to recommend mercy for Hannah. Was this because of her sex, or did they think that Con had struck the actual blows and that Hannah, although guilty in law as a participant, was involved only in helping her brother dispose of the body?

When the judge asked Con O'Leary whether he had anything to say as to why sentence of death should not be passed upon him, he replied, 'I had not hand, act or part in the murder.' He was then sentenced to death, the date for his execution being fixed for 28 July 1925. Con then repeated what he had said, adding, 'I am going to die an innocent man.' When the judge asked Hannah O'Leary the same question, she answered in a strong, clear voice, 'I did not kill my brother.' Both the accused appealed, but without success.

Three days before her brother's execution date, Hannah O'Leary was reprieved, and the Government commuted her sentence to life imprisonment. She was detained in Mountjoy Prison, Dublin, until 18 September 1942, when she was released on licence to enter a convent.

Cornelius O'Leary was executed on 28 July 1925.

4
A Triple Killing Down Under

If ever there was a man who had all the odds stacked against him almost from birth, then John Desmond David, who lived in the Australian state of Victoria, was that man.

During the Second World War John's father was away from home serving in the Army, so they saw very little of each other. At this time, John was at just the age when a boy most needs a father's influence. The absence of a father at this time has of course been a feature of life for many boys, whether caused by the exigencies of war or by other factors, but in most cases the boys have managed to survive this emotional deprivation.

As if this were not enough, John's mother abandoned her family of three boys and two girls, of whom John was the eldest. His father obtained compassionate leave from the Army and returned home in order to place the children in various homes and institutions. He had no other choice, for he had no relatives who could care for the children, and those few relatives his wife had all refused. He could not give up his Army career as it was his livelihood. After he had reluctantly farmed out his family, he then rejoined his unit, which was sufficiently far away to preclude visits to his children more than once or twice a year. Predictably, the older children, including John, were resentful of what they saw as abandonment by both parents, not being old enough to understand the problems their father faced.

John David saw very little of his brothers and sisters and eventually lost touch with them altogether. They had been placed in widely scattered homes, not by choice but because there was no room for five children in any one place, nor even for more than two, so they ended up split up into three homes. John was the 'odd man out' and the two homes where his four siblings lived were hundreds of miles from the one where John resided.

John was not only deprived of a normal family life, but he was also abnormally short in stature. Too tall to be termed a dwarf, he was only five feet tall in his shoes even when he was a fully-grown adult. A man who was not even of average height could hardly present a macho image to the world, and where a man of normal intelligence would have at least a fair chance of coming to terms with his physical shortcomings, perhaps by compensating intellectual attainments, John had an IQ at the lower end of the dull to average range. He was barely able to read and write. Always a loner, he became more and more introspective.

As soon as he was old enough to leave school – which had been able to do little for him – he was placed in work by the institution in which he was living. Because of his low intelligence and lack of educational attainments, he could be no more than an unskilled labourer, and was sent to work as a general labourer on a farm. But after only a day or two, he was returned by his employer to the institution. He had been ready and willing to work, but he was too small to do the heavy work required. He was placed out on another farm, with the same result. He was given a trial in other forms of employment which required labouring duties, but with no other success than in farm work. He was unfitted to do anything except menial labour, but too small to do the heavy work involved.

John became more and more embittered and resentful, but eventually he was found a job as an assistant to the gardener who looked after the grounds of a hospital in Melbourne. He mowed lawns, did weeding, dug and manured flower beds and cleared rubbish to be burnt in the garden incinerator. He managed to hold this job for some time – encouraged, no doubt, by the fact that he had met a ward maid at the hospital. Four inches taller than John, she felt a strange affinity with this shy, introspective young fellow who rarely spoke unless spoken to. Eventually they decided to marry, and for the first time in his life John David had happiness and security within his grasp. The couple had two children, and now John was able to capture some of the joys of family life which he had never known.

John and his wife and children rented a house in Croydon, a Melbourne suburb, and in order to be able to work nearer home he left his job at the hospital and obtained work as a cleaner at a drive-in cinema in the Croydon suburban area. He bought an old car, and when he made use of his special privilege as an employee of being able to take his wife to see the current movie free of charge, the toddlers would sleep in the back of the car. Every Friday he gave most of his pay packet to his wife, leaving himself only a small sum for petrol, beer and other incidentals. At this time he was not a heavy drinker. But he was happy and contented with his new-found family life.

Suddenly the bottom dropped out of his world. It was May – winter in Australia – and attendances at the drive-in movie theatre had dropped to an all-time low. The management decided to make most of the staff redundant, leaving only those who were indispensable. The first to be given their cards was John David. After all, the management's thinking ran, anybody can clean the place. We can double up the cleaning work with the usherette. She'll do both jobs if we increase her wages a bit as an inducement.

The manager called John into his office, explained the position, and handed him, along with his cards, three weeks' pay in lieu of notice plus his accrued holiday money, plus his usual week's wages. This was more money than he had ever had in his whole life.

Unemployed, the insecurity that had haunted John in the past now returned, intensified, perhaps, because he had latterly known a different kind of living where he had what he had considered to be a secure job with its regular money coming in to support his family. He was afraid to tell his wife that he had been made redundant, and he handed over only the usual weekly amount of housekeeping and kept the rest.

On the following Monday, 24 May, he left the house, ostensibly to go to work, at the usual time. In his pocket was the money he had received, minus the one week's housekeeping he had given his wife. He bought a .22 rifle – which he had always wanted to own – and some ammunition, and spent the day shooting at rabbits or practising on moving targets such as bottles floating down the fast-flowing Yarra River near Wonga Park, a secluded spot on the outskirts of Melbourne. In summer it was a popular picnic spot, but now in winter it was deserted.

The next day, Tuesday 25 May, he again went off at the usual time in the morning, his wife suspecting nothing of her husband's job loss. In his battered old car he drove around aimlessly for a while, his old resentments and frustrations building up within him. At about 11 a.m. he stopped in the industrial suburb of Fitzroy and went into a hotel, where he ordered a couple of beers and got into conversation with Janice Freeman, a twenty-six-year-old drifter with a free-and-easy lifestyle who sat drinking alone at the bar. She was not averse to accepting the offer of another drink from the short stranger who, she sensed, was probably as lonely as she basically was herself under her easygoing exterior.

When John asked Janice to go for a drive with him into the country she readily agreed. He bought a six-pack of beer, and they drove off to a remote place in the bush known as Woori Yallock, about thirty miles from Melbourne. They sat together in the front seats of the little car drinking the beer and talking.

At some point in the conversation, Janice made what John considered to be a derogatory remark about his wife. His reaction was instantaneous. Reaching under the seat, he pulled out the loaded rifle and shot Janice dead as she sat in the passenger seat. He then pushed the body out of the car and threw out all the beer bottles, both full and empty, indiscriminately. Then he drove back to Melbourne and went home at the usual time he came home when he had been working. His behaviour was perfectly normal, as if nothing had happened.

The next day, Wednesday May 26, John again left home at his usual time, and drove off to Wonga Park, the place where he had first practised shooting after he had acquired his gun. He decided to shoot at anything that appeared to be a good target. He was walking about, looking for rabbits or anything else, when he saw a young couple ride past on a scooter. They were Neil Bray, a nineteen-year-old university student, and his girlfriend Linda Spinks, aged eighteen, who was a student teacher. They had come to the park for a winter picnic, carrying a camping cookstove, frying-pan, bangers and tomatoes, bread and apples. Linda was a keen swimmer and the lower winter temperatures did not deter her as she changed into a swimsuit behind some shrubbery, leaving her clothes and handbag a little way from the river bank.

John could not resist the temptation of looking in the bag for money, but Neil spotted him and shouted out. John dropped the bag and ran off. Neil was more than six feet tall and rapidly closed the distance between them; even Linda was only a short distance behind. John was still holding his rifle. Wheeling round, without warning he shot Neil dead. Linda screamed and started running towards Neil's body. As she did so, heedless of the danger, she, too, was dropped in her tracks by John's deadly .22.

John left the bodies where they lay, returned to his car, stowed the rifle under the seat and drove around various Melbourne suburbs for the remainder of the day until it was time for him to return home.

The next day he again left home at the usual time. One wonders how often he thought about what he would do when his money ran out. How then would he be able to keep up the pretence to his wife that he was still working? And even now, while he had money, he would have to start fabricating some good excuses when his wife reminded him that Friday was their free night at the movies.

News of the seemingly inexplicable and motiveless shooting at Wonga Park filled the morning papers with banner headlines. John decided to return to Wonga Park and watch the police at work on their investigation. He moved around quite openly, tagging along behind the police as they searched for clues. Inevitably, his obvious interest aroused the curiosity of the police, and they asked him a few questions about his own movements at the time of the shooting. His evasive answers were unconvincing. The police decided to examine his car, and found the .22 under the seat. It was the same calibre as the weapon that had fired the fatal shots.

Quite quickly, John unburdened himself to the police, and told them the whole story. After giving the police details of his killing of the young couple, he gratuitously told them of his first murder at Woori Yallock. Janice Freeman had not even been reported missing, and this was the first the police knew of it. She was a free-wheeling hitch-hiker who would take off for weeks at a time and then just as suddenly return to her usual haunts. Her sudden disappearance was wholly in character for this footloose girl, and her friends never even began to imagine that anything untoward had happened to her.

John took the police to Woori Yallock and led them to the

spot where he had pushed Janice out of his car. Her body lay, still undiscovered, where he had left it.

John David's trial went before one of the most experienced judges in Australia, Sir John Barry. He made a full confession, during the course of which he stated that he did not wish to raise any question of a defence of insanity, and went on: 'My counsel [Philip Opas, QC] has advised me that there is no available evidence to support such a defence and, indeed, that all available evidence from psychiatrists engaged on my behalf negatives insanity ... In any event, I consider that when the killings took place I knew what I was doing in that I knew I was firing a rifle loaded with live cartridges at a person and that there was a certainty, if such a person were struck [that] he or she would be at least seriously injured, if not killed. I also knew that such action on my part was wrong ... I am extremely sorry for what I have done and I want to make atonement for my actions by pleading guilty. My life up to now has not been any credit to me and at least I want it to be said that I did not try to bluff my way out of my actions by pleading not guilty ....'

After John David's confession had been accepted by the court, the Crown Prosecutor, Mr J.S. Mornane, called the prison psychiatrist, Dr A.A. Bartholomew, to depose as to the defendant's mental condition. The doctor confirmed that John David was not suffering from any mental illness or psychosis, and that his only defect was a dull level of intelligence, but notwithstanding this he understood the nature of the court proceedings perfectly adequately.

Mr Justice Barry then asked John David whether he had anything to say before sentence of death was passed, to which he replied in a firm voice, 'No, sir.' The judge then pronounced the death sentence.

It would be another ten years before the State of Victoria abolished capital punishment in 1975. While John David languished in his cell, resigned to his fate, the government council appointed to review all capital cases before sentence was carried out decided to grant him a reprieve, in the light of the mitigating circumstances of his harsh upbringing in impersonal institutions, his lack of any family life before his marriage, his constant difficulty with employment owing to his low educational and intellectual achievements, and his inferiority complex as a result of his abnormally short stature.

All these, they decided, could have been factors that had contributed to the explosion of frustration and resentment which had resulted in the killings. But, according to the M'Naghten Rules, which state that a person is legally sane if he or she knows what he or she is doing and knows that it is wrong, John David was perfectly sane. They commuted his sentence to twenty-five years in prison.

5

Murder at the Opera

In the ornate Vienna State Opera House preparations had begun at 4 p.m. for the evening's scheduled performance of Wagner's *Die Wolküre* (The Valkyrie). At about five o'clock Gertrud Galli, a twenty-two-year-old hairdresser employed by the opera company, entered the ladies' shower rooms at the top of the building. The eerie stillness of the deserted showers contrasted sharply with the bustle of the stage below. Opening the door of the lobby to the showers, Fräulein Galli was met by a horrifying sight. On the floor lay the body of a little girl with long blonde hair, almost naked, covered with blood. The hairdresser was too petrified even to scream. She ran to notify the janitor, who called the theatre company's doctor. He confirmed that the child was dead, apparently from multiple stab wounds.

The victim, ten-year-old Dagmar Fürich, had been a student at the opera ballet school for two years. On the afternoon when her body was found, slender and frail-looking Dagmar had left her home at 22 Boltzmanngässe to attend a ballet rehearsal scheduled for 5 p.m. At six o'clock opera-lovers were watching that evening's performance of the brooding tale of murderous gods, unaware that a real murder had been committed backstage.

While the opera progressed, the body had still not been removed as the police began their probe behind the backdrop curtain. One of the very first to arrive on the scene was a tall, distinguished-looking man with silver hair who could easily have been mistaken for a diplomat. He was Dr Friedrich Kuso, chief of the Vienna State Security Office and Austria's most renowned detective.

The little girl's body lay on its back, the legs pulled up and the left arm stretched out. On her left wrist was a small gold watch which was still working so it could not be used to pinpoint the time of the attack. Her blue blouse with white mother-of-pearl buttons and her pink slip, both saturated with blood, had been pushed up under her arms. Her white underpants, black knickers, light brown ballet tights and beige stockings had all been pulled down to her ankles, leaving most of the body naked. Brown buckled shoes were still on her feet. A blue knitted cap, a blue pleated skirt, a blue cardigan and multicoloured scarf lay folded nearby. In the pocket of a grey winter coat with a brown fur collar which was hanging from a clothes-hook was a ticket for a No. 6 bus dated for that day – 12 March 1963 – and a key. A plastic handbag containing sweets and a pair of woollen gloves lay on a bench.

The entrance to the shower lobby was blood-spattered, as was the adjacent row of radiators. There were more bloodstains on the wall above the bench, below a bolt on the inside of the door and on the light switch, and on the wall nearby were wiped blood smears. There was a large pool of blood under the body.

According to the autopsy, the left side of the child's chest had been stabbed seventeen times through the clothing. Of these wounds, thirteen had pierced or touched the heart and left lung and had penetrated the posterior chest wall. The fact that the stabs were so close together led the pathologist to the conclusion that the killer had not pulled the murder weapon out completely after each major thrust. Ten of the seventeen stabs had penetrated the back of the rib cage and passed through the clothing. The police had already noted that seven of these thrusts had even damaged the floor beneath the body, four of them going completely through the floor covering, indicating the ferocity of the attack and the strength of the killer.

The pathologist was able to state that all seventeen of the stabs to the chest were inflicted before death. There were also five stabs to the left temple, three of which had penetrated the brain. These five wounds were apparently inflicted after death. The actual cause of death was massive haemorrhage from the chest wounds which had penetrated the heart. There were eleven further stabs in the genital area, two of which had penetrated right through into the abdominal cavity ending at the spine. One of them had pierced the bladder.

The murder weapon had been a hunting-knife or similar

type of knife with a firm but fairly long and slender blade. Before the infliction of the fatal wounds there had been an attempted strangulation and blows to the face and head. The child had not been raped or otherwise sexually molested, apart from the stab wounds in the genital area, which clearly marked the killer as a sexual psychopath.

The search for the murderer set in motion one of the most massive manhunts in European criminal history. Kuso was only too aware that a homicidal psychopath frequently blends indistinguishably into the normal populace when he is not on one of his murderous rampages. He is usually an ordinary-looking person whom one would not look at twice. If he is a schizophrenic, it is unlikely that he will show any perceptible signs of guilt or apprehension; he may even be quite unaware of his homicidal outrages when he is in one of his 'normal' phases.

Kuso was in a dilemma while the opera was still in progress, which hampered his investigations. Not a single fingerprint had been left behind by the killer. The investigators did, however, manage to come up with some clues. The impression of a rubber-soled shoe was found on the floor of the shower room, and blood smears were found on the doors to the main floor of the Opera House and also on the inside of the glass of the stage door leading on to Kärntnerstrasse, the street behind the theatre.

Kuso's team searched the Opera House with police dogs for more than twenty-four hours without success. All exits were put under police guard, and as the investigation continued teleprinter messages were despatched informing all law enforcement agencies in Austria of the murder.

Soon after the killing, other ballet students were questioned. One, eleven-year-old Susanne Fichtenbaum, said that while ascending the staircase at 4.15 that afternoon she had seen a man in front of the glass door on the second floor, whom she had greeted. He had then turned and descended the stairs towards her, answering her greeting in the same way. She had passed him, and then when she had reached the third floor she looked down at him, because she had noticed that he seemed nervous and had what she described as 'a frightening appearance'. She then observed that he was ascending the stairs again. She thought he was lost and was about to ask him which part of the building he was looking for, but thought better of it. She described him as approximately forty-two years of age, about 1m 72cm (5ft. 8in.) tall, with wavy dark blond hair combed back. She said that he was wearing a grey suit and carried a black briefcase under his arm, which gave her the impression that he was an office employee.

Subsequently several persons reported to the police that at about the time of the murder they had seen a man leave the Opera House by the Kärntnerstrasse exit. A good description was given by a salesman named Ludwig Kovacs, a Hungarian, who stated that on 12 March while he was driving behind the Opera House at about 5.15 p.m. a man had 'run across the street like crazy', as he put it, from the direction of the Opera House. He was of medium height, thin, without an overcoat (unusual in March), dressed in a suit, and had 'protruding eyes'. In his haste he had paid no attention to the heavy traffic and had narrowly escaped being hit by a cab.

Kuso and his investigators set about trying to reconstruct Dagmar Fürich's last moments. The ticket found in her coat pocket showed that she had boarded a No.6 bus at 4.15 and had alighted in the Kärntnerstrasse at the stop known as the Opera House stop at about 4.31 p.m. Dagmar should therefore have reached the Opera House at its Kärntner-strasse entrance at about 4.33 p.m. Using a girl of the same age, Kuso's officers reconstructed Dagmar's walk from the bus stop to the shower rooms, from which they concluded that she must have met her killer at the very latest by 4.38 p.m.

Dagmar's coat was hanging on a hook, the fastening of her pleated skirt was not torn, and her handbag had been placed on the bench and her cardigan and other items neatly folded. This pointed to the conclusion that she had gone to take a shower and started to undress, leaving her clothes tidy, and that her killer had entered while she was undressing.

Kuso was sure that the murderer was familiar with the Opera House layout. He could therefore be a member of the opera company, or associated with it in some way perhaps as a janitor or cleaner. Inquiries revealed that there was very little control over entry into the building, and this could quite easily have enabled a complete stranger to familiarize himself with its interior. There had also been group tours through the

Opera House; these usually started at the main entrance in Operngässe, continued across the staircase on the second floor which led past the scene of the crime, and ended at the exit in Kärntnerstrasse. Employees revealed that during these guided tours male visitors not infrequently separated themselves from their groups by some ruse and were later caught as 'Peeping Toms', looking at female artistes in the showers and dressing-rooms. However, to avoid a scandal the opera authorities had never reported these incidents to the police; when they caught these men they would just give them a stiff warning.

Kuso decided that the investigation could not be limited to the opera company personnel only; still, the employees of the State Opera, who *in toto* numbered approximately 1,900 individuals, could scarcely be ignored, and Kuso and his investigators interviewed each and every one of them. They ranged from the artistic personnel – soloists, chorus singers, ballet-dancers, musicians, extras – to technicians – stage-hands, scene-shifters, prop-makers, wardrobe handlers, hairdressers, stage-dressers, make-up experts, cleaners, ticket-sellers and security staff – and also of course included the Opera's administrative personnel.

Employees of several firms which had been engaged in street construction work in front of the Opera House prior to the murder were also questioned. The investigations also included the checking of known sex offenders and the evaluation of prisoners who had been released on parole as well as former mental patients who had been discharged. Interpol was also asked to make inquiries abroad. A check was also made for the possibility of any escapes from mental hospitals. Dry-cleaning establishments were questioned about any bloodstained clothing, and cutlery stores about anyone purchasing a knife, based on measurements of the wounds and the supposed shape and form of the murder weapon. Possible suspects reported by the public were followed up. During the probe Kuso and his sleuths conducted no fewer than 14,000 interviews. But still the psychopathic killer of Dagmar Fürich remained at large.

Prof. Dr. Grassberger, chairman of the Institute of Criminology at the University of Vienna, consulted by Kuso, confirmed that tracking a homicidal psychopath is one of the most difficult tasks that can face the police. He pointed to three famous German cases – Haarmann, Kürten and Lübke – recalling that these three men had all committed a long series of murders over several years before they were apprehended, and that all were caught only by a sheer fluke in each case. Grassberger expressed the opinion that despite the massive search so far it was quite possible that another murder would occur: the question was when and where?

Kuso and his colleagues did not have long to wait. True, it was not a murder, but it was a serious attack. On 17 June 1963 at about 6 p.m. a twenty-six-year-old student named Waltraud Brunner, together with her friend Liselotte Fremuth, went to a movie. As the two girls entered the darkened cinema, Fräulein Brunner felt a blow on her thigh just as a man passed her and ran out. An usherette, Herta Wendler, thinking that the fellow had rudely pushed the girl aside in his haste, chased him, but he escaped. The two girls took their seats in the cinema, and only then did Fräulein Brunner notice that her dress was becoming soaked with blood. She had been stabbed in the thigh. An ambulance was called, and a cut measuring 1½ cm (½in.) deep was found. She said that the man had been around 1m 75cm (5ft. 9in.) tall, but could not give any further details owing to the darkness of the cinema. The usherette described him as about 1m 65cm (5ft. 5in.) tall, slender, with dark blond wavy hair and dressed in a dark coloured ski jacket and dark trousers.

During the course of that summer it was all too tempting for the media and even the police to voice the opinion that another Jack the Ripper was loose in Vienna. On 30 July at about 3.40 p.m. a twenty-two-year-old American student on holiday in Vienna named Virginia Cioffi visited the historic Church of St Augustine in the city. She was sitting in one of the rear pews when a man came down the aisle and without warning grabbed her, seized one of her breasts and punched her in the right eye, knocking off her spectacles. He then picked up the glasses, threw them at her and ran out. The terrified girl fled from the pew towards the High Altar at the opposite end of the church. Then her assailant turned round and came back into the church, caught up with her and stabbed her several times with a knife, all the time without uttering a single word. He then fled.

In response to her cries a tourist guide named Jakob

Wiellandt and a woman who was waiting to be guided round the Habsburg burial vaults rushed to her aid. While the woman took care of the wounded girl, the guide ran outside to look for a policeman. The assailant had escaped.

An ambulance took Miss Cioffi to hospital and Kuso was immediately notified. At his request the chairman of the University of Vienna's Institute of Legal Medicine, Prof. Dr Leonard Breitenecker, came into the casualty ward and examined the girl's injuries even before the doctor on duty had time to treat them. There was a contusion from a blow to the outer edge of the right eye, and her right earlobe was cut through. There was a puncture in the area of the right collar-bone, a puncture in the left breast and two punctures in the right side of the back. One of these stabs had only narrowly missed the heart. An immediate search was launched for the attacker, who Miss Cioffi described as being between twenty-eight and thirty years of age, 1m 75cm (5ft. 9in.) tall, slimly-built, with blond hair combed back and a slightly tanned face.

Even while this police investigation was being pursued, a third knife attack on a woman took place. On 2 August a forty-one-year-old saleswoman, Frau Maria Brunner (no relation to Waltraud Brunner) closed her tobacco kiosk on Praterstrasse shortly after 7 p.m. On her way home she was taking a short-cut through the Stadtpark and sat down on a bench to rest for a while during the warm summer evening. She had been sitting there for about forty-five minutes when suddenly she felt a blow on her neck. As it was already dark and she could not see, she thought children playing had hit her with a ball. She took no notice and continued sitting there. A little later she rose from her seat and walked towards the park exit which leads towards Weihburggässe. On the way she passed a woman sitting on another bench. This woman, seventy-three-year-old Frau Rosa Turkoff, told Frau Brunner that she was bleeding. She also pointed out a man heading for the Weihburggässe at a smart trot. Only then did Frau Brunner realize that she must have been stabbed in the neck and not hit by a ball. She was taken to Vienna's general hospital, where doctor found that a wound in the right side of her neck, 18cm (7in.) in length, had punctured her right lung.

The man seen leaving the park, despite the fact that it was

dark, was described in some detail by Frau Turkoff – about 1m 72cm (5ft. 8in.) tall, slenderly-built with dark blond hair combed off the face – the description was becoming sickeningly familiar, although the estimates of his age varied. Kuso was notified of this latest assault and despatched squad cars full of officers to scour the area, but the phantom knifeman had seemingly disappeared into thin air.

By now, alarm was understandably beginning to spread throughout the city, which was agog with rumours of this second Jack the Ripper. Women were now much more careful where they walked, especially after dark, and looked warily over their shoulders for strangers dogging their footsteps. Kuso ordered reinforced park patrols and redoubled his efforts to round up and question known sex deviates and others about whom his investigators had received information. The mysterious knifeman, however, continued to elude them.

As Kuso had anticipated, the assailant would ultimately trip himself up during the commission of one of his crimes. This was brought about on 6 August by a respectable elderly woman, sixty-four-year-old Frau Emma Laasch, who arrived home from her job at about 4.50 p.m. and entered the hall of the block of flats where she lived. As she opened her purse to take out her key, a hand reached out from behind her and clamped itself over her mouth. At the same time she felt what later turned out to be a stab in the right side of her neck. She wrestled free and found herself looking at a man holding a dinner-fork in his hand.

Frau Laasch managed to elude her assailant, who fled when she screamed for help. With great presence of mind she ran after him, and observed him running into a building in the next block, Truchlauben No.5. She told passers-by what had happened, and one of them called a traffic policeman, Johann Kowaryk, who entered the building and ran up the stairs. Between the second and third floors he encountered a man who was flushed and perspiring as though he had been running. When the officer questioned him as to what he was doing in the house, he gave evasive answers, which aroused the patrolman's suspicions, so he took him into custody.

The fugitive was Josef Weinwurm, a thirty-two-year-old native of Haugsdorf, Austria, who stated that he was employed as a salesman. Was this fork-wielding mugger the same man as the knife-wielding attacker of the Stadtpark? Could he be the man who had attacked Virginia Cioffi, Maria Brunner, Waltraud Brunner? Could he be the sex-crazed psychopath who had killed little Dagmar Fürich? There were certainly some similarities in the *modus operandi* of all these crimes, but Kuso was far too astute an investigator to jump to conclusions. Moreover, there were many who did not believe that Weinwurm, who was suspected of being an amateur burglar and mugger, could possibly be also the random knife maniac who evidently stabbed women for kicks.

Kuso and his fellow-detectives began a painstaking check into Weinwurm's background, and discovered an interesting series of patterns. Weinwurm, who had stated that he was a salesman, was in fact unemployed, a drifter with no fixed address. He turned out to be an ex-convict with a police record. Delving more deeply into the court records of his numerous convictions, mainly for burglary and other theft-related offences, Kuso discovered that a large proportion of Weinwurm's burglaries had been committed in dressing-rooms and cloakrooms, including the dressing-room of a skating club, an actor's dressing-room in the Löwingertheater, the dressing-rooms of the Gösserbierklinik and those of the Kleinestheater, the cloakrooms of the Opernkino (a cinema), and several other similar places. Kuso had also received a communication from the prison governor where Weinwurm had last been incarcerated that a knife had been found among his belongings on two separate occasions.

Kuso was quick to realize the significance of Weinwurm's penchant for burglarizing dressing-rooms and his predilection for knives, and although this amounted to circumstantial evidence rather than actual proof, Kuso considered it more than mere coincidence, and thought that Weinwurm could very well have been the man who had committed the savage murder of the little ballet student. Kuso was, however, far too shrewd a detective to reveal such a potential trump card prematurely, and his officers, in their initial interrogation of the suspect, studiously avoided any reference to the Opera House murder, confining their questions to the series of assaults on women that had occurred subsequently.

In the immediate case at hand – the attempted hold-up of

Frau Laasch with a dining-fork, Weinwurm denied being the man responsible. However, a black jacket, proved to be Weinwurm's, had been found abandoned on one of the landings at No.5 Truchlauben. He was made to put on this jacket and then confronted by his intended victim, who immediately recognized him as the man who had attempted to rob her at her front door.

On 7 August, the day after the attack on Frau Laasch and the apprehending of Weinwurm, Virginia Cioffi was released from hospital. A police line-up of suspects, not including Weinwurm, was shown to her, but she eliminated all of them. She was also shown mugshot books which did not include Weinwurm's photograph, with the same result. Next, Miss Cioffi was taken to inspect another police identity parade, this time including Weinwurm, and on this occasion Miss Cioffi positively identified him as her assailant. Other witnesses also identified him as the man seen leaving Vienna's Stadtpark after the stabbing of Maria Brunner. The movie theatre usherette, Herta Wendler, picked him out as 'probably' the man she had chased after the knife attack on Waltraud Brunner. Yet, despite all these damaging denunciations, Weinwurm continued to deny all knowledge of the attacks, pleading mistaken identity. Kuso, or one of his associates, interrogated him daily, but Weinwurm steadfastly maintained his innocence, and refused to give police any details of his movements or whereabouts after his last release from prison.

Kuso now made a personal appearance on TV and appealed to the public for help, asking Austrian citizens to come forward with any information they might have about the life of Josef Weinwurm, however insignificant they might consider it. This plea proved more successful than Kuso had dared to hope.

Two waiters from a café recognized Weinwurm from a newspaper photograph. They told Kuso about another waiter who was a frequent companion of Weinwurm, a fifty-four-year-old man named Ernst Gschellhammer, who had a long police record. Picked up and questioned by Kuso, this man admitted that he had met Weinwurm in Stein Prison in 1960, and that since the preceding Easter Weinwurm had been living with him without registering his address with the police, as ex-convicts were required to do by law.

For four months Gschellhammer had been sheltering

Weinwurm in his small one-room apartment without the knowledge of his landlady. The latter had a full-time job, and Weinwurm used to leave in the mornings after she had gone to work, spend the time wandering around the city (his 'salesman's job' was a myth) and then return under cover of darkness after the landlady had gone to bed. Since Weinwurm supported himself by burglary he was understandably anxious to conceal his whereabouts. Gschellhammer was sentenced to a token sixteen days in prison for harbouring an ex-convict without revealing his address to the authorities. But at least now the police knew why they had been unable to find Weinwurm during the spate of stabbing attacks in the city.

Kuso now decided to drop casual remarks about the Opera House murder into his continuing interrogation of Weinwurm about the attacks on women. Weinwurm strenuously denied that he had been anywhere near the Opera House on the day in question, and still kept up his complete denial of involvement in the stabbing attacks. He seemed to be quite immune to long continued days and nights of questioning. However, he readily admitted to a string of burglaries.

Kuso let his suspect sweat it out in custody under the continuing barrage of relentless questioning. Then, suddenly, the break came. It was totally unexpected, as often happens in cases of this kind. On 27 August Weinwurm requested a confidential meeting with a certain detective who had shown some degree of sympathy towards him. To this detective Weinwurm confessed not only to all the assaults on the women but also to the murder of little Dagmar Fürich. He then made a long statement describing the murder with details that only the killer could have known, and stated that he had lured Dagmar, totally unsuspecting, into the shower room by posing as a doctor and telling her that he was examining all the ballet students. He told her to take off her clothes, which she did, and at that point he made his ferocious fatal attack upon her.

Running from the Kärntnerstrasse exit, he told of his having been nearly run over by a cab, thus corroborating the evidence of Ludwig Kovacs, the salesman-motorist, which was known only to the police and had never been made public. The cab-driver was also found and confirmed that he had narrowly avoided hitting a man who had been running 'at a fast speed' from the Opera House exit. Weinwurm also divulged things which, although not in the official report, clearly fitted perfectly into the web of circumstantial evidence. For example, he had visited the Opera House four days before the murder, intent on burglary, and stolen a purse containing forty schillings from a choirmaster's room. This was later confirmed by the man concerned, who had never mentioned the matter to anybody, as he did not wish to cast any aspersions on his colleagues.

After his escape from the scene of his crime, Weinwurm made his way to the Schweizer Gate and the Hofburg (Vienna's former Imperial Palace). There he slipped unobserved into the building and hid his bloodstained coat and gloves behind some boxes on the second floor. Police found them there, exactly where he had said they were. This was incontrovertible proof of Weinwurm's involvement in the murder, and without such tangible proof he might have been able to retract his confession, as so many murderers do.

As the motive for his crimes, Weinwurm declared, 'I hate all women.' When it was pointed out to him that little Dagmar Fürich was not yet old enough to be described as a woman, Weinwurm stated that he had gone to the Opera House intending to find a woman to kill, but found only the small girl available. 'She was female,' he said. 'She would have grown up to womanhood if I had not stopped her.' Psychiatrists who examined him were of the opinion that his avowed hatred of women masked a hatred for his mother, who had continually urged him to give up burglary, find a decent job and lead a respectable life.

In the asylum where he is incarcerated, a decent job has been found for him keeping stock of the laundry; there is nothing worth burgling, and he has to lead a respectable life – he has no other choice.

6

The Cabin in the Woods

No one looking at the mild-mannered, even shy young man who lived quietly with his wife in California would ever have imagined him capable of committing the hideous murder of a teenage girl. Slightly-built, bespectacled and studious-looking, his name was Burton Abbott (called Bud by his friends, after the comedian) and he had a lot going for him: a sense of humour and above-average intellect, a mastery of the game of chess, and a flair for *haute cuisine* cooking. Only physically did he fall short of the healthy image of the all-American boy. Born in San Francisco in 1928, he was tubercular from childhood, and by the time he reached his teens he had had one lung and several ribs removed. His parents encouraged him in outdoor pursuits, in order that ample fresh air might aid his recovery.

After graduation from the University of California he married another graduate he had met there while both were majoring in accounting. Her name was Georgia, and she was older than her husband. For some unknown reason, Georgia decided soon after their marriage that she would prefer to work in a beauty parlour rather than an accountants' office, and obtained a position as a beautician with Leona Dezman, who owned a prestigious beauty parlour in the city. Bud, however, preferred to stick to his accountancy career.

The couple lived an exemplary life, were active in their neighbourhood church and community projects, and were never short of money. Bud still kept up his outdoor pursuits – fishing, small game hunting and rock scrambling, for which the ideal locale was the Trinity Mountains. He was still somewhat frail in health from residual tuberculosis, and the mountain air was just what he needed to maintain his health. He bought a home in Alameda, which was within commuting distance of his job in Berkeley, and also purchased a cabin in a wooded part of the Trinity Mountains. He would drive the several hundred miles north of Alameda to his cabin on most weekends. Georgia was not at all keen on hunting, fishing or rock-climbing, and preferred to stay at home and entertain her friends or visit local places of interest while her husband indulged in his more strenuous pastimes.

One day – it was 28 April 1955 – a fourteen-year-old girl vanished, seemingly into thin air, off the street in front of the Hotel Claremont in Berkeley. She had been walking a classmate home from their high school. When she did not arrive at her own home at her usual time, her parents became anxious, since it was quite out of character for the girl, Stephanie Bryan, to be late home from school unless there were some good reason such as a school function to attend after classes, in which case she would invariably telephone home to inform her parents. It was not long before they decided to report Stephanie missing to the police.

The missing girl's parents convinced the police that their daughter was not the type to run away, or even to go and spend the night with a girl friend without asking their permission first. She was not the type to hang around boys, or to dabble in drugs. So the police took the girl's disappearance seriously and initiated a search. Several reports came in of seeing a young girl with a man in a car, but the reports differed in their descriptions of the girl, the man and even the car, except that all were agreed that the man was 'young'. How young is young? He could be a teenager or he could be thirty. Most witnesses are notoriously inept at estimating a person's age, especially in a moving car. The police were stymied. How could they put out a BOLO (be on the look-out for) a car they did not know the make, year or even the colour of, or for a man whose only known characteristic was that he was young? As for the girl, they hadn't a clue. Most of the witnesses had told them that they *'thought* they saw a girl in the car'.

Thirteen days later, on 11 May, a backpacker hiking in remote Franklin Canyon found a French textbook bearing Stephanie Bryan's name and the printed logo of her school. The book was processed for fingerprints, but any it had borne had been wiped clean. It was a complete mystery as to how the book had turned up in such a remote spot, but it lent credence to the theory that Stephanie had been abducted by a man in a car.

On the evening of 15 July, Bud Abbott was entertaining a friend in his home, Otto Dezman, the husband of his wife's employer. After dinner, Georgia Abbott served coffee, and then turned her attention to preparations she was making to put on a play she had written in the community centre. She needed some costume material, and remembering that she had several boxes of old clothes and other materials in the basement, she went down the stairs and rummaged among them. Buried under old clothes in one of the boxes, she found a wallet which she knew had not been there previously. Intrigued, she examined the wallet, which she could see contained several items, by the light of the single naked electric light bulb that illuminated the basement. The wallet contained an ID card bearing the name Stephanie Bryan, several photographs of the girl's high-school classmates, and an unfinished letter she had been writing to a girl friend. The letter was dated 28 April 1955 – the day Stephanie had vanished. Georgia Abbott was an avid follower of local items in the newspaper, and realized immediately that the wallet she had found belonged to the missing girl. She rushed up the stairs, all thought of her play forgotten, and showed the wallet to her husband and Dezman who were sitting at table still lingering over their coffee. 'This wallet belongs to that girl who's still missing!' she cried. 'How on earth could it have gotten into our basement?'

'I think we should call the police,' Dezman said. 'Maybe they can find out.'

When police arrived, Bud was just setting out the chessmen in readiness for a game with Dezman. The officers took possession of the wallet and agreed that it had indisputably belonged to the missing schoolgirl. The officers asked the couple and their guest a few routine questions, but no one seemed to have any ideas as to how the wallet had turned up in their basement, particularly since their house was situated in Alameda and the girl had gone missing from Berkeley. The officers made a few notes, left the premises, and Bud and Dezman returned to their interrupted game.

The following day the same two officers returned with a search warrant and went over the entire basement with a fine toothcomb. Bud sat at the kitchen table engrossed in a crossword while Georgia was cooking.

While the officers were searching the basement again from

top to bottom, one of them spotted a patch in the earthen floor which looked as though the soil had been recently disturbed. He started digging, and had not gone very far when he discovered the missing girl's school-books and her brassière. Her name was on the brassière as well as the books – girls at her school were required to have woven name-tapes sewn into all their clothes which were left unattended in the cubicles while the pupils were having swimming lessons in the pool.

Confronted with this fresh evidence, Bud shrugged and said that anybody could have hidden the items in the earth floor and also buried the wallet in a box of clothes in May when his garage had been used as a polling-station and any number of people could have gained entry to his basement, which adjoined the garage and opening into which was a good-sized window in the garage wall. For some inexplicable reason the police never bothered to check this window to see whether there was a layer of undisturbed dust on the ledge, which would quickly have put paid to the idea of someone scrambling through. Satisfied with this plausible explanation, they went away convinced.

It was left to a newsman to discover what had happened to Stephanie Bryan. Following a hunch, Richard L. Wright, a reporter on the local newspaper, took one of his friends and two hunting dogs and visited the cabin in the woods in the Trinity Mountains, about which there had been considerable publicity following Abbott's questioning by the police. Photographs of Abbott had appeared in his hunting gear carrying a rifle and accompanied by his two pointer dogs, Ricky and Starr. The cabin had appeared in several photographs, along with details of its location. It had never been investigated by the police, possibly owing to the fact that it was the best part of 300 miles from Abbott's home.

Wright and his friend loosed their dogs, which quickly rushed to one spot and started nosing about and then frantically digging. The two men leashed the dogs, fetched a spade from their car, and began to dig. Soon they had uncovered a shallow grave, in which the badly-decomposed but still recognizable body of Stephanie Bryan lay, her head crushed and strangled with her own panties. The body was naked.

An inquest was held after the autopsy had been

performed; the coroner could not be certain that Stephanie had been raped owing to the advanced stage of decomposition of the body, but he considered it was extremely likely. He opined that the head injuries had been inflicted with a heavy blunt object such as a rock in order to subdue the victim when she resisted. He speculated that the killer had strangled the girl afterwards to prevent her reporting the rape to the police.

Bud Abbott was arrested, charged with unlawful kidnapping and murder. His trial was a long-drawn-out affair, massive circumstantial evidence being piled up against him, but he appeared to take the whole matter very lightly, even laughing when the prosecutor alleged that Abbott had intended to rape Stephanie, beaten in her skull when she resisted, and strangled her afterwards to silence her. The jury was very unimpressed by his behaviour when he took the stand, where he did not improve his chances. After the seven-day trial, he was found guilty of murder in the first degree by a unanimous verdict, and sentenced to the gas chamber in San Quentin.

On death row in the prison he was granted several stays of execution, some for only hours, while appeals were frantically prepared by his attorneys. All these appeals were quashed. Even such outspoken anti-capital punishment campaigners as Supreme Court judge William O. Douglas and Edmund G. Brown, then Attorney-General, rejected his pleas. Abbott continued to plead not guilty, even in the face of the most damning evidence.

Shortly before the day set for his execution he was visited by the San Quentin prison psychiatrist, Dr David Schmidt, who asked him to tell him the truth about the killing, since he was going to die anyway. 'I can't admit it, Doc. Think of what it would do to my mother. She could not take it,' he replied.

But Abbott never made a formal public confession of guilt, and went to his death on 14 March 1957. At 11.15 a.m. the lethal gas was released, and as the deadly fumes rose in the chamber a telephone call was received by the prison governor from California Governor Goodwin A. Knight asking him to stay the execution yet again. The prison governor replied that it was too late, as the gas had already been released. The stay of execution would have been only for one hour anyway, and the reason for the stay was never explained, at least not publicly.

By 11.25 a.m. Bud Abbott, namesake of a comedian and hunting and fishing expert who had owned a cabin in the woods, was dead.

.

7

In the Name of Allah

Still in California, we have another University of California student, a brilliant young man with an IQ of 140 who taught himself to read at three years of age and had read hundreds of books by the time he was eight years old. But this student was as different from Burton Abbott as it is possible to imagine. His studiousness and his academic achievements – he had graduated head of his class at fifteen – belied the instability of his nature from childhood. At only nine years of age he had tried to hang himself, and only a few years later he tried to burn down his parents' home after a violent argument with his mother. He was committed to Camarillo State Hospital, where psychiatrists diagnosed him as a schizophrenic and recommended an extended period of psychiatric care as an in-patient, but upon his apparent improvement he was released. He was asked to attend the hospital once a week as an out-patient for psychiatric counselling, but turned up to only the first two appointments.

The boy's name was Joseph Howk, and he was the only son of respectable hard-working parents, who raised him in the Roman Catholic faith. His father was white, his mother black. He was born in 1939 at Long Beach, California, and attended Long Beach City high school where he amazed his teachers with his mental abilities. On graduating at fifteen he went to Long Beach City College, from which he obtained a scholarship in 1958 to the University of California in Berkeley. In only two years he majored in Near Eastern languages and Islamic culture, being the youngest student ever to gain a degree in these subjects.

Two years earlier, much to his parents' dismay, he renounced the Roman Catholic faith and embraced Islam. He changed his name to Mohamed Abdullah. At college he had nurtured Nazi sympathies, which made him very unpopular. Although tall and handsome, with brown eyes and jet-black hair, no girl would dare be seen talking to him because of his pro-Nazi views. By the time he entered university, however, he had undergone a complete volte-face. No longer pro-Nazi, he became an ardent, even fanatical devotee of the Muslim faith, and even wore a fez and carried a prayer mat. He frequented beatnik coffee-houses – it was the era of Haight-Ashbury (the part of San Francisco where the original Hippies tended to live or meet) and the Flower Children – and in one of these student hang-outs he met and befriended a drifter, Martin Horowitz, thirty-four years of age, who had dropped out of high school and spent the last eighteen years in and out of various mental institutions. He was considered an eccentric by the students who frequented the coffee-houses. The two became inseparable until 1959, when Joseph – whom we should now call Mohamed – met Sonja Hoff, a twenty-one-year-old statuesque blonde beauty majoring in home economics, intending to take up social work after graduation. Sonja was fascinated by minority groups, and this may have encouraged her to associate with Mohamed. Sonja also needed help in learning the Persian language, at which Mohamed was brilliant. He volunteered, and tutorship deepened into love. But Sonja little knew how jealousy would affect her already unstable and unpredictable boyfriend ....

He would only have to see Sonja talking innocently with another student, and he would fly into an uncontrollable rage. In his diary entry for 6 April 1960, after seeing Sonja talking to another student, he wrote: 'Tonight I tried to kill myself, but Sonja put herself between my knife and my throat. Next time I suspect her of liking another man I shall kill her quickly and without warning.' But Sonja chose to ignore the danger signs, and she still continued her affair with the man who carried a knife and uttered threats at the slightest provocation.

Just two weeks later, Mohamed saw Sonja talking to another student. She was merely discussing which textbooks she could borrow from the university library. Mohamed rushed up to them and in a loud voice threatened to murder her. Police were called, who ordered him off the campus, but he did not leave the town. In fact his threats against Sonja continued unabated, and he extended these to include an Iranian student whom she sometimes dated. At the end of the semester she left town, but returned in July to take a vacation job as a waitress in a restaurant adjoining the campus. On 11th July Mohamed spotted her in the restaurant where she was working, and begged her to come to his apartment, where he secretly planned to cut her throat and then kill himself by putting his head in the gas oven. She refused.

Frustrated in his purpose, Mohamed went to see his friend, Martin Horowitz, who, he knew, had a gun, and begged him to lend it to him. Asked why he wanted the gun, Mohamed gave the unlikely explanation that the mere possession of a gun and his knowledge that he had it in his power to commit murder would distract him from the actual deed and soothe his tensions! In later statements he claimed that he had stolen the gun from Horowitz, and still later that he had bought it from him. Horowitz, displaying a complete lack of any sense of responsibility, handed a loaded .38 pistol to his unpredictable and unstable friend, whose violent temper, he knew, had a short fuse. But whether he had borrowed, stolen or bought the gun, it ended Sonja Hoff's life just the same ....

On 13 July 1960 Mohamed went to the University library (ignoring the ban on his entering any part of the campus), borrowed a typewriter and typed a lengthy confession of the murder and suicide he intended to commit. 'In the name of Allah,' the confession began, 'I have stolen a pistol to kill my beloved and myself ....'

Leaving the confession in the typewriter, he then walked into the main reading room of the library and went up to Sonja, who was seated at one of the tables studying, and asked her to step outside where they could talk. Incredibly, the girl did as he asked her, with no thought of the number of threats he had made against her life. 'I love you, Sonja,' he whispered as they walked together along the corridor and out on to the steps outside the entrance to the library building, where he whipped out the gun and shot her at point-blank range, killing her instantly with one bullet to the head. He fired a second shot at her as she fell, but missed. He then shot himself in the head. But he did not die; the bullet lodged in his brain and blinded him in the right eye. He was taken to hospital, where surgeons worked to remove the bullet. After his recovery, he was sent for trial charged with the murder of Sonja Hoff, and Martin Horowitz, too, was charged with manslaughter, albeit by remote control.

Mohamed Abdullah was sentenced to die in San Quentin's gas chamber, and said that he wished to die in this way. However, his death wish was not destined to be granted, for California Governor Edmund G. Brown, whom we met briefly in the last chapter, commuted his sentence to life imprisonment without possibility of parole. His friend Martin Horowitz was sentenced to ten years in the same prison, but the record does not say whether they were able to keep up their friendship behind San Quentin's grim walls.

8

The Burden

Hopetoun Quarry is situated in a secluded spot in a remote part of West Lothian in Scotland, about a mile east of the village of Winchburgh and nearly half a mile north of the main road to Edinburgh. It is surrounded on all sides by clumps of trees and thick brush. The quarry is about a hundred yards in length and forty yards across, and is about forty feet deep in the middle, the dark waters shadowed by the overhanging trees, giving it a sinister and menacing appearance. It is seldom visited – few people know of its existence – and it can be reached only by a muddy cart-track.

One Sunday morning in June 1913 two ploughmen out for a walk stumbled across the little-used path and decided to explore to see where it led. The quarry, then as now, had fallen into disuse. As the two men came out of the dark, wooded path the quarry lay before them; not a ripple broke its surface. Jack Summers, the younger of the two labourers, spied a dark object near the bank, floating on the surface not far from where they stood.

'Look, Pete!' he cried. 'A scarecrow some chap hae thrown in for a joke!'

But Peter Aitken, his older companion, was suddenly filled with a sense of foreboding. A cold tremor went through his slim frame, although it was a warm, sunny day. 'I'll wager that's nae joke,' he replied somberly. 'That's a human body, for sure.'

'Ye canna be serious!' said Jack. 'Let's take a look.' And, so saying, he picked up a fallen tree branch from the ground and hooked the object on to the bank. 'Jesus Christ!' he breathed. 'It's twa wee bairns!'

The two small bodies were tied together with window-sash cord. They were fully-dressed, grotesquely bloated from long immersion in the water, and their facial features were unrecognizable. Their clothing was rotting, though both appeared to be dressed alike. As Jack pulled them further up on the bank out of the water by hooking the branch under the sash-cord, it had rotted to such an extent that it broke under the strain. The ploughmen did not stop to investigate their find further but retraced their steps as fast as the boggy terrain allowed, and went to fetch a policeman.

The tiny bodies were taken to the mortuary at Linlithgow, to await the arrival of the forensic pathologist, Sydney Smith (later Sir Sydney) and Professor Harvey Littlejohn, who held the Chair of Forensic Medicine at Edinburgh University. They were to perform the autopsy.

The post-mortem revealed that the two bodies had been in the water from eighteen months to two years, having been during the course of such long immersion almost wholly transformed into adipocere. This is a hard, fatty substance of a whitish colour produced in a corpse by a chemo-physical change in the body fat occurring after death when the body is immersed in water, or buried in damp soil. This conversion is a slow process, but permanent when complete. It is fairly rare for dead bodies to be found which have become completely transformed, and this case was exceptional, as the entire bodies had been so transformed into adipocere, except for the feet which had been encased in leather boots and thus protected to a large extent from the action of the water on the tissues. The case was of great interest to the forensic scientists from a purely medical viewpoint, apart from any other considerations such as how the two children had met such a dreadful fate.

The clothing had, as Jack Summers and Peter Aitken had observed, almost rotted away, but as the pathologists removed the garments from the bodies it was apparent that both victims had been dressed alike, in shirts, serge knickers, T.O.T. (turn-over-top) stockings with elastic garters, and black leather boots. The underwear was too disintegrated to be recognizable. The clothing was of a very cheap quality, suggesting that the victims had been in poverty-stricken circumstances. This surmise was soon proved correct as Sydney Smith deciphered the official stamp of the Dysart Poor Law Institution on the back of one of the shirts. So they had been children of the workhouse.

The external features of the bodies were too distorted to

enable age or sex to be determined with accuracy, but an internal examination established that they were both male, and measurements of their bones and the condition of their teeth seemed to point to the boys being about seven and four years of age. It seemed highly likely that they were brothers.

An astonishing fact emerged which was to prove of great assistance in discovering the boys' identity. The extensive adipocere formation had preserved the stomach and its contents intact, and it could be shown that their last meal, which had consisted of Scotch broth, easily recognizable from its traditional constituents, some of which were in a still undigested state, had been consumed not more than an hour before death. This suggested that the children had lived locally, or at least that they had not been brought any great distance to this lonely spot. No vehicle could negotiate the cart-track across the moorland bog to the quarry, and it was the opinion of both pathologists that the two boys had walked to the quarry with their murderer. Most likely, therefore, the murderer was a person the boys had known well enough to accompany him – or her – on their last walk. He – or she – was probably a relative. Perhaps an aunt or uncle? Or even a parent?

The police, now that they had some details to go on, set about searching their files for reports of missing children in the preceding two-year period. They discovered quite soon that two little boys, one aged nearly seven and his four-year-old brother, had unaccountably vanished from the neighbourhood in November 1911. Their father, a widower, had been in prison for failing to maintain them.

Patrick Higgins was born in Scotland, the son of Irish immigrants who had come looking for work. He was an ex-soldier who had married a Scots girl. He had worked at the Winchburgh brickworks as a labourer. Their first son, William, was born in December 1904, and the second, John, in August 1907. Higgins was a heavy drinker and neglected his family; his wife took a job to support herself and the children as her husband spent all his wages on drink. She was of frail health, and died in 1910. At first the widowed father received poor relief from the Inspector of Poor – a sort of pre-First World War social security, the forerunner of the dole. But Higgins wasted this money in taverns and neglected the two boys, who went hungry and ill-clad. The

Inspector therefore ordered their removal into care at the workhouse in Dysart, Fife.

The parish authorities, who controlled the workhouse, applied to Higgins for payment of maintenance for his children, and when he refused to pay he was committed to prison for two months. On 24 August he came out of prison, and two days later he collected the boys from Dysart Poorhouse and brought them back to the Winchburgh district, where he boarded them out with a widow named Elizabeth Hynes, whom he had known since he was a boy, who lived in the next village of Broxburn. He returned to his work at the brickyard, and lived the life of a dosser, sleeping rough – sometimes in a shed at the brickworks – and cooking his meals over an open fire, using his spade as a frying-pan and his bucket as a soup-canteen. He was noted for his dirty and unkempt appearance, and spent his entire wages of twenty-four shillings a week on drink.

Although he promised Mrs Hynes that he would pay for his sons' keep, he never gave her a penny. She informed the Inspector of Poor, who went to see Higgins at the brickworks and threatened to take the children away again and send him to prison for failure to maintain them. Higgins then took the boys to the brickworks, but was told by his foreman that he could not keep them there. The next night, a wild and stormy November evening, a miner named Hugh Shields saw Higgins walking away from the brickyard with the two children across the moors, and the children were never seen again.

Hugh Shields was in the village pub when Higgins returned, alone, that same night. Asked where the boys were, Higgins told the miner that he had arranged for a friend to put them on the next ship to Canada.

This was but one of the many fanciful stories Higgins told various acquaintances regarding the boys' whereabouts. Another miner, James Daly, who had known Higgins since he was a boy, was told that 'two ladies he had met on a train had decided to adopt them, as they had no children of their own'. Another miner, Llewellyn Richards, was told a similar story, while a brickyard workmate, Alexander Fairnie, was told a version which, though substantially the same, varied somewhat in minor details. Later Fairnie, on inquiring after the children, was told that they had been accidentally drowned in another part of Scotland, and Mrs Hynes, meeting Higgins in the street some time after this, was told that both the boys had been drowned in Canada in a boating mishap.

The police, meanwhile, wasted no time. Slowly but surely they built up the case against Higgins. More and more persons were found who were able to recall various versions of what Higgins had alleged had become of the boys. Some said that he had told them he had put them in an orphans' home or in a residential school. The chief wardress at Dysart Poorhouse identified the shirts worn by the bodies when found. The police even succeeded in finding a woman who remembered giving the boys their last meal of Scotch broth, on a cold and rainswept evening at the beginning of November 1911.

Within a few days of the finding of the bodies Higgins was arrested, while staying with the widow of Broxburn, at two o'clock in the morning. He was lying on a couch, fully-dressed even to his boots, in a downstairs room, a blanket thrown over him, having come in late the previous night very much the worse for drink. Four policemen took him, unprotesting, into custody. He showed no anxiety or concern, and when asked where his boys were he said that he did not know. He was charged with their murder, and when cautioned had nothing to say.

The trial took place in Edinburgh three months later. The prisoner sat expressionless in court, and appeared quite unconcerned even when he stood in the dock on the capital charge.

Although it was proved that Higgins had been discharged from the Army on the grounds of epilepsy, the opinion of the last defence witness, Dr G.M. Robertson, was that this was a good many years previously and that the accused had apparently had no fits for some considerable time, and that he was a sane man with no mental disease but that he was mentally unbalanced by alcohol.

Lord Johnston, the trial judge, after a careful review of all the evidence, in his summing-up told the jury that their verdict must depend on whether they considered that Higgins was sane at the time the crime was committed. Witnesses who had seen him with the boys on the day they were last seen alive were agreed that Higgins was definitely not drunk at that time and walked in a perfectly sober and normal manner.

The jury retired for an hour and a half, and then returned for further directions from the judge on a series of legal points. They then retired for a further forty-five minutes, after which they returned a unanimous verdict of guilty as charged, with a recommendation to mercy owing to the length of time that had elapsed between the murder and the trial.

A profound silence enveloped the court as the verdict was announced. Higgins heard his sentence without betraying the slightest sign of emotion. He stood to attention in soldierly fashion, and remained calm as he was led down to the cells.

There was no reprieve. His execution was set for Wednesday, 21 October 1913. Shortly before the time he was due to hang, the prisoner, who was a Roman Catholic, received Holy Communion in his cell, and Mass was said in his cell by Canon Stuart of St Mary's Catholic Cathedral.

After Higgins had gone to his account, Canon Stuart stated that he had been calm to the last and had walked steadily to the drop. He had previously told the Canon that he wanted it to be known that the sentence was just, and that drink had been his downfall to ruin.

The two perfectly preserved specimens of adipocere transformation were taken to the Forensic Medicine Museum at the University of Edinburgh, where they are to this day. They are still used to illustrate adipocere formation to students of medical jurisprudence, and probably will for many years to come.

9

The Body in the Street

Hume Street, Dublin, is situated in the well-known Georgian area of the city, off St Stephen's Green, one of the city's finest squares. In April 1956, when our story opens, most of Hume Street was let out in flatlets and bedsitters, catering mostly to respectable middle-class folk, with a fair sprinkling of the elderly and retired – what one would call a quiet neighbourhood. Not the kind of neighbourhood where one would expect to find a dead body lying on the pavement ....

Early in the morning of 18 April the first person believed to have noticed anything unusual was a Mr Gleeson, a milk roundsman, who was delivering milk just after 5 a.m. when he saw what he thought was a bundle of clothing lying partly on the pavement and partly on the steps which led down to the outside basement area of No.15. Busy with his deliveries, he paid no further attention to what appeared to be someone's discarded rubbish, beyond thinking that the pavement was an odd place to dump one's old clothes. In about fifteen minutes he had completed his deliveries, and departed in his van.

At about 6.25 a.m., a Mr Patrick Rigney, another milk roundsman, was driving his milk float into Hume Street from St Stephen's Green, and he too saw the bundle of clothing which had earlier attracted Mr Gleeson's attention. But as Rigney drew nearer, he saw two legs protruding from underneath a black overcoat, and realized that it was a woman's body. The head was covered by a skirt, the black overcoat covering the remainder of the body, which was also clothed to the waist but nude from the waist down. There was a stocking tied loosely around the woman's neck, and her legs were tied together above the knees with another stocking and also a torn pair of knickers.

On the fifth step down into the basement area there was a

parcel containing, among other things, a lady's handbag and a pair of women's shoes. On the pavement nearby was a mark about three feet long, indicating that some object had been dragged along the footpath as though to sweep it clear of the obstruction. This mark led from the head of the body towards the front steps of No.17, which was two doors away from No.15 outside which the body lay. The houses in Hume Street were numbered consecutively.

The Gardaí were summoned without delay and arrived almost immediately. A nursing sister was called from the nearby hospital, and confirmed that the woman was dead. When she tried to raise one of the woman's arms which lay across her chest, she was unable to do so because the arm was stiffened in rigor mortis. The time was noted at 6.32 a.m.

At 8.20 a.m. the state pathologist, Dr Maurice Hickey, arrived and examined the body, which was subsequently transported to the City Morgue, where Dr Hickey later performed an autopsy.

The dead woman was aged about thirty and had been about five months pregnant. She had undergone an illegal abortion. Death had been caused, in the pathologist's opinion, by an air embolism, which had stopped the circulation of the blood. Unconsciousness would have occurred about fifteen seconds after the insertion of the instrument which had caused the air embolism, and death would have ensued not more than two minutes thereafter. If the findings of the pathologist were correct, then the Gardaí almost certainly had a murder case on their hands ....

Who was this woman who had died in this dreadful way and whose body had been dumped like so much garbage in the public street? All identification had been removed from her handbag, and only the usual feminine accoutrements remained such as a powder compact, lipstick, and a purse containing a few coins. There was no door key. All labels had been cut from her clothing, including the black overcoat and even from the insides of the shoes. It was obvious to the Gardaí that whoever had killed her had been at pains to prevent her from being identified.

Inquiries discovered that strange sounds had been heard emanating from No.17 Hume Street in the early hours of 18 April by a Mrs Farrelly, who lived in a two-roomed flatlet on the first floor of the house. She was awakened at 5 a.m. by noises which sounded to her like 'dragging or pushing something, moving furniture, perhaps'. The noises came from the landing outside her door, and from the stairs down to the ground floor. The sounds continued until nearly 6.30 a.m., stopping for about five minutes before Mr Moran, one of the other tenants, could be heard passing her door and walking down the stairs on his way to work at 5.45, his usual time. After Mr Moran had left, closing the front door behind him as quietly as possible in accordance with his usual practice, the noises then continued.

No one else in the house had heard these disturbing noises, nor had any of the tenants moved any furniture during the night. However, corroborative evidence was provided by another person in a house two doors away, at No. 15. A Mr James Kirwan, who lived in the first floor flat and whose bedroom was at the front of the house, stated that he had heard a noise outside in the street below which sounded like someone pushing a broom along the pavement. The sound was continuous, not intermittent, but it stopped twice, and lasted altogether for about six or seven minutes. He could not pinpoint the time of night when he had heard the sounds, except to say that 'it must have been after 3.30 or so as it was beginning to become daylight'.

The Gardaí continued to question the tenants of all the houses in the immediate vicinity. At No. 17 a retired midwife, Nurse Mary Ann Cadden, aged 62, occupied the rear room on the first floor, the door to which was almost opposite Mrs Farrelly's door. The nurse no longer practised midwifery, but had one or two private patients whom she treated on a regular basis for ailments such as rheumatism, fibrositis, sciatica and so on with manipulative therapy. Most were elderly men. Asked whether she had seen or heard any unusual noises during the night or early morning, she replied, 'I could not have heard any noise. My room is at the back of the house. Anyway, I had the radio on all night, as I suffer from arthritis and it had kept me awake.' This statement, however, differed from what she had told Mrs Farrelly, who had asked the same question: 'No, I never heard anything; I was fast asleep in bed.' When Mrs Farrelly insisted that there had been considerable noise, Nurse Cadden then said, 'It must have come from next door.'

When the Gardaí told the women about the dead body that

had been discovered outside, Mrs Farrelly crossed herself and exclaimed, 'God bless us! Is it known who she is?' while Nurse Cadden said, 'Isn't it terrible?' and then, almost as an afterthought, added a curious remark which, in the light of subsequent developments, was to have a good deal of significance: 'It must have been a man who did such a thing!'

The state pathologist had noticed the distinctive odour of disinfectant emanating from the body. A bucket in Nurse Cadden's room emitted a similar odour, and since the nurse was contradicting herself all the time on interrogation, the Gardaí were becoming suspicious. They decided to obtain a search warrant.

'Search if you want to,' the woman said with the utmost *sang-froid*. 'You will not find anything here.' The search took some time, for the Gardaí were thorough. Behind a bookcase filled with volumes on human anatomy and other medical topics, two syringes and a pair of forceps were found, along with two lengths of rubber tubing, which fitted on to the ends of the syringes. When asked their purpose, the nurse explained that she used them for giving enemas. When the Gardaí asked her why they had been thus hidden, she replied, 'They're hardly the kind of thing to keep on show!'

In a hat-box on top of the wardrobe, wrapped in a white cloth, were two speculi (a speculum is an instrument used for examination of the womb). When the Gardaí lifted the hat-box down, Nurse Cadden said, without any prompting, 'That hat-box has not been taken down for years.' But fingerprints in the dust on the lid belied her. On being shown the speculi by the Gardaí, she said, 'I had these when I was working in the nursing home at Rathmines.' The nursing home in question had been closed in 1939 ....

The Gardaí took all these items, together with two rubber sheets and a couple of strong spotlight lamps such as are used for surgical examinations, and also Nurse Cadden's black-covered diary. She was then asked to account for her movements on 17 and 18 April, to which she replied, 'Of course – why not?' She said that from 2 p.m. until 7 p.m. on 17 April she stayed in bed, as her arthritis was very bad. She then rose and made some tea, and went to Mrs Farrelly's place for a chat. She was there about twenty minutes. She then went back to her room and to bed, where she stayed until about 10.30 p.m., saying that her arthritis was giving her 'a lot of bother'.

At about 10.30, Nurse Cadden continued, her doorbell rang, and rather unwillingly she rose, dressed again hurriedly, and went downstairs. The caller was one of her male patients. She told the Gardaí, rather unconvincingly, that she could not remember his name, although she had been treating him on a regular basis for a stomach complaint. Asked whether it was her custom to treat patients so late at night, she said that this particular man had a long way to travel and he could not get to Dublin any earlier. 'I think he comes from Kilkenny,' she added lamely. Kilkenny was seventy-five miles distant.

This somewhat curious narrative was flatly contradicted by Mrs Farrelly's version. She told the Gardaí that to her certain knowledge Nurse Cadden had been in her own room talking with two women during the afternoon and had not been to see her at all. In the evening, she said, Nurse Cadden was up and down the stairs to and from the sink on the landing doing a lot of washing and drawing water.

Further questioning of Nurse Cadden was conducted to ascertain where she was during the night of 17 to 18 April. She averred that she had held a consultation with her patient referred to above until about 11.30, when she said he left to stay in an hotel as he could not get home that night. She then went back to bed, and said after taking some more of her tablets her arthritis eased off somewhat and she managed to stay sound asleep until 8 a.m. when she was awakened by the postman's knock. She said that he knocked only for the ground floor tenant, whose doorbell did not work. She said that she heard no noises of any kind during the night. The Gardaí then left.

A week later the Gardaí were back again, this time to question Nurse Cadden about her diary which they had taken away on their last visit. Before commencing his interrogation, Superintendent Lawlor, who had been studying certain entries in the diary, cautioned Nurse Cadden that she was not obliged to answer any of his questions, but she answered them willingly enough. He wanted her explanation of a diary entry dated 17 April, the day before the body was found. The entry had been made almost illegible by heavy overwriting and ink markings across the writing of the original entry, and by the use of two different coloured inks, red and blue. Nurse Cadden stated that the entry read, '2 p.m. Blue coats', which meant that two patients wearing blue coats were to call at that hour for treatment, but in fact they had not turned up. She repeated what she had told the Gardaí in a previous interview, that she never kept a note of her patients' names, and several anonymous entries in the diary seemed to bear this out. A strange practice indeed for a qualified professional nurse ....

Superintendent Lawlor suggested that the original entry had been 'Black coat' and had been overwritten to make it indecipherable. Nurse Cadden replied that this was not the case and that her pen had merely run out of red ink and she had gone over the entry to make it clearer. It was certainly not clear – it was practically illegible.

Superintendent Lawlor then asked Nurse Cadden to explain an entry dated 30 March, which stated merely '£50'. This certainly required some explanation from a nurse whose fees varied from three shillings to twelve shillings and sixpence. She said that the fifty pounds was for 'professional services rendered to several members of the same family over a period of time'.

Nurse Cadden made a number of other contradictory statements. When asked further about her late-night caller, 'I spoke to him,' she said, 'about his arthritis, and also about cortisone ... I did not know who he was until I went to the door to let him in. Then I recognized him as one of my patients I had not seen for some time. I was going to give him some drugs, but I was feeling very fatigued and asked him to come back again some other time, although he had come from nearly 200 miles away to see me ... He has not called back since.' She insisted that she did not know the man's name.

The discrepancies in Nurse Cadden's two statements about this patient were remarkable. From a stomach complaint he had now switched to arthritis, and had come from 200 miles away instead of Kilkenny. Instead of giving him an hour's consultation from 10.30 to 11.30, she now said she had as good as told him to go home as she could not treat him. She also said he had come without an appointment, although she had previously told the Gardaí that she never in any circumstances saw patients without an appointment.

The lino on the floor of the entrance hall to the house, a carpet on the landing outside Nurse Cadden's door and some mats in her room were taken away for forensic examination, and all were found to bear traces of human blood. A small spot of human blood was also found on the forceps which had been taken from her room by the Gardaí on a previous visit.

The flagrant contradictions in Nurse Cadden's various statements had already enmeshed her in a web of confusion. She flatly denied that she had been carrying water or washing anything on the evening of 17 April, although she had been seen doing so by Mrs Farrelly. More suspicious evidence, which would be aired at the subsequent trial, came into the hands of the Gardaí as their investigation proceeded, and on 27 May 1956 they arrested Nurse Cadden and charged her with the murder of the unknown woman. 'I'm not saying anything,' she replied. 'I'll tell it to the judge.' And in the district court, at the preliminary hearing, when asked if she wished to say anything, she replied, 'I have nothing to say, only that I deny the charge.'

The trial opened on 22 October 1956 and lasted ten days, three of which were taken up by the evidence of forensic pathologists. The judge was Mr Justice McLoughlin; prosecuting were Mr Desmond Bell and Mr James Ryan, while Nurse Cadden was defended by Mr Ernest Wood and Mr Noel Hartnett. The murder charge stood because if the accused had performed an illegal abortion, which is a felony, in consequence of which the woman died, it would be murder, even though she had not intended to kill. The killing of a person during the commission of a felony is murder, regardless of intent.

Mr Rigney, the milk roundsman who found the body, in addition to what has already been stated earlier, said that a few minutes before he entered Hume Street and found the body he had been proceeding in the direction of St Stephen's Green, and when passing the end of Hume Street he observed a woman on the footpath at the spot where he later found the body. The woman, he said, was crouching over something – he could not make out what – on the pavement, and as his vehicle passed she turned her head, and he noticed that she wore spectacles. Although it was dark, he could see the glint of the lenses. She was of stocky build, and seemed to be wearing some kind of white garment such as an overall. Later, when he found the body, he heard a sound from below, and leaned over the railings to look down into the basement area. He said that a woman was in the area standing with her back to the wall and looking up at him. Asked whether he could give a description of this woman, he said that he could not remember anything except that she was wearing glasses. He was then asked whether he thought it was the same woman that he had seen previously on the footpath, he replied that he could not be certain. He repeated, however, that he was sure she wore spectacles. Questioned further as to why he was so sure of this, he said that it was because she had been looking up straight at him. It is curious to a degree that he was not asked to give his estimate of the woman's age, since if she had looked up at him he would have had a full-face view of her.

Mr Wood next questioned Mrs Farrelly about the voices of the two women she had heard coming from Nurse Cadden's room. Mrs Farrelly had gone out that afternoon and, returning about an hour later, the voices of the two women, she averred, were still audible. Mr Wood suggested that she could not be sure that she had heard the voices of two different women in addition to the voice of the nurse, and that if she had, she could not possibly be sure that they were the same two an hour later. Mrs Farrelly, however, could not be shaken on this point. Yet she had made an extraordinary mistake when the Gardaí had asked her, on 18 April, whether she had heard any sounds in the night. At first she had said no; how, then, had she come to forget the 'pushing and dragging noises' she had mentioned earlier? She was seventy-four years old, which might, perhaps, have accounted for her lapse of memory ....

When Nurse Cadden's diary was produced, a police photographer gave evidence of photographing and enlarging the entries under various dates, including the one for 17 April. By the use of a filter, he was able to obliterate the black overwriting, and succeeded in producing a photograph which showed only the original red ink entry, which clearly read '8 p.m. Black coat'. The result was deadly: now the jury knew incontrovertibly that Nurse Cadden had an appointment on the night before the body was found with someone wearing a black coat, and had tried to conceal the fact. It could point to only one conclusion ....

The individual witness whose evidence took the longest

was Dr Hickey, the state pathologist, who spent two days in the witness-box. He said that the syringe, without the nozzle and rubber tubing attached, was in common medical use, but with those attachments it could cause an injury of the same kind as that suffered by the deceased woman. He considered that the insertion and use of the syringe, as so adapted, would require some skill to avoid injury to the cervix or vagina, neither of which bore any marks of injury. Asked about the age of the bloodstain on the forceps, he said it was comparatively fresh – not more than one month – and that there was no way it could have remained on the instrument since the accused alleged she had last used it in the course of her duties at the Rathmines nursing home, which had been closed for seventeen years. There was, however, no way of determining the blood group of this stain as it was too small in size. The other instruments taken from the accused's room had not borne any bloodstains.

Dr Hickey described the skin of the body and some of the deceased's clothing as scraped, scratched and grimy, suggesting dragging over a dirty or dusty surface. This tended to confirm the evidence of Mr James Kirwan, one of the tenants at No. 15, mentioned earlier in this account. Dr Hickey confirmed the time of death as between 9 p.m. and 3 a.m. – well after the time of the appointment in the accused's diary.

Numerous hairs and fibres had been collected by the Gardaí from Nurse Cadden's room and from the dead woman's clothing. Human hairs do not serve to establish identity, but it could be said that some found in the room and on the clothing were similar, suggesting that the deceased had been in the accused's room, but this was not conclusive. Under microscopic examination, fibres found in the room similar to fibres found on the deceased's coat suggested the same thing, but again, this was not conclusive evidence.

Another pathologist, Dr Stanley Earle, had collected samples of loose hairs and fibres at random from the footpath between Nos. 10 and 19 Hume Street, and also from a broom in Nurse Cadden's home. Many of these, too, were similar.

When the prosecution's case closed, Mr Wood, for the defence, applied to have the case withdrawn on certain legal grounds and also for what he considered to be lack of conclusive evidence, but the judge refused the application.

Mr Wood made a magnificent six-hour effort in his speech to the jury on behalf of his client, followed by Mr Hartnett who was to close the case for the defence. With such a difficult case, based as it was on circumstantial evidence, he was as convincing as he was able to be. His valiant efforts turned on such fine points as whether Mr Rigney could have seen the glint of light on spectacle lenses at 6.25 a.m., when it was not yet daylight and in fact the sun would not strike Hume Street until 8.30 a.m. The basement area would have been in deep shadow, Mr Hartnett averred, and it is unlikely that Mr Rigney, or anybody else, could have seen such a glint as the milkman had described. A fine point indeed ....

Mr Hartnett was puzzled as to why Mr Rigney had not spoken to the woman he saw in the basement area who, he had alleged, was looking up at him. Why had he not asked her, 'What's happened up here? Did you see anything?' or some similar remark. It would have been the normal thing to do. After all, Mr Hartnett continued, the woman lying on the pavement might only have been drunk, or have had an epileptic fit or a heart attack, or even just fainted. Mr Rigney could have asked the woman to help him tend her, or call an ambulance from the nearby hospital.

After the judge's summing-up, the jury was out for only one hour before returning with a unanimous verdict of guilty of murder as charged. The judge sentenced her to be hanged on 27 November 1956, and when asked if she had anything to say on why sentence of death should not be passed, she replied, 'You will never do it!' adding, somewhat curiously, 'Well, I am not a Catholic.' Outside the court, feelings were running high, and a large crowd had gathered in the street. As soon as the verdict was made known, shouts of 'Murderess!' and 'Hang her!' went up.

An appeal, based mainly on legal points at Mr Wood's instigation, failed, but Mary Ann Cadden's prophecy, 'You will never do it!' proved to be correct. Her solicitor, Mr Stanley Sieff, lodged a petition to the government pleading for clemency, and her sentence was commuted, on 4 January 1957, to penal servitude for life. No woman had been executed in Ireland since 1925, and Nurse Cadden may have thought she could safely assume that she would not hang.

Life in prison for Mary Ann Cadden proved to be short. In August 1958 she was transferred from Mountjoy Prison to the Central Criminal Mental Hospital at Dundrum, Co. Dublin, where, on 20 April 1959, she died of natural causes.

And the unfortunate woman whose body had been found in Hume Street? From that day to this, she has never been identified.

10

More Deadly than the Male

While Nurse Cadden did have professional nursing qualifications, Nurse Jane Toppan did not. Both women were called 'Nurse' but there the resemblance ended.

Jane Toppan was an adopted child. The Toppan family lived in Lowell, Massachusetts. Jane had the usual kind of upbringing normal in a respectable middle-class family. She went to a school which had a good reputation for its pupils' academic achievement, and quickly joined the ranks of the gifted, being described as an above average student in all subjects and in particular an excellent pupil in religious studies. By 1882, when she left school, Jane had decided to make her career in nursing, and enrolled for a two-year nurses' training course in a hospital in Cambridge, Massachusetts. There she quickly gained the approval of her tutors on account of her eagerness to learn. It also did not go unobserved that the promising young student nurse took an inordinate interest in post-mortem procedures.

During the course of her training, Jane, like all the other probationers, had to do a certain amount of practical work, involving the actual nursing of patients under supervision. It so happened that two of Jane's patients died while in her care, for no apparent reason. Acting under pressure from the relatives of these patients, the hospital decided to terminate Nurse Toppan's training. They could not afford to take any chances, or risk a scandal caused by keeping incompetent or careless girls on the course.

Not to be daunted by this setback to her career, Jane Toppan applied for, and obtained, a post as head nurse at another hospital, claiming qualifications which she did not possess. Quite soon, the hospital discovered that her alleged qualifications were bogus, and dismissed her summarily.

Jane Toppan was not the kind of girl to be put off her chosen career by two such disasters in a row. She now decided to fulfil her vocation by looking after the sick in their own homes. This would be without the benefit of formal qualifications, but many of these private patients did not demand them anyway. She was now twenty-six, and there was no time to be lost. So she became a private nurse, which she found very rewarding. There was less drudgery and more 'perks' than on a hospital ward.

Nurse Toppan was highly regarded and considered a caring person, working for many families in America's New England states. The odd one or two patients died, of course, but that was only to be expected when so many of them were elderly and bedridden. 'When they're over 80', Nurse Toppan is on record as having told a woman friend, 'a lot of them don't want to live anyway. What pleasure can it be for them stuck in bed day in and day out?'

In 1901 Nurse Toppan, moving on once again, was tending the Davis family, who lived in Cataumet. Mattie Davis, the family's mother, was terminally ill, and Jane Toppan had been engaged to look after her. She died early in the summer. A married daughter came to stay with the family from Chicago, but she never made it back home. She was stricken by a mysterious illness, characterized by distressing symptoms and agonizing pains, which failed to respond to the medicine Nurse Toppan administered. The sick woman tried to refuse the medicine, since it was not doing her any good. 'Sister knows best,' Jane said as she held the glass to the woman's lips. Within hours the patient was dead.

The husband of Mattie Davis, father of the daughter from Chicago, was the next to die. This left Jane alone in the house with the second married daughter, whose husband, a Captain Gibbs, was away at sea. Mrs Gibbs was, quite naturally, feeling very despondent at having lost no fewer than three members of her family in a matter of months. 'My dear, you look absolutely terrible!' Nurse Toppan said as the two women sat drinking coffee in the kitchen a few days after Mr Davis's funeral. 'Let me give you a tonic.' The nurse went to her medicine chest and poured some concoction from a green bottle into a medicine glass, adding a little water. The unprotesting Mrs Gibbs drank the mixture despite its bitter taste. 'I only hope it does me some good,' she said. 'It tastes absolutely foul.' The next day, Mrs Gibbs had gone to join her departed family.

It was now time for Jane Toppan to move on yet again to a new nursing assignment. In the meantime, Captain Gibbs had returned from his ship, and was horrified to learn what had happened to his wife and her family. He wasted no time but sought a court order for the exhumation of his wife's body. It was found at the autopsy that Mrs Gibbs had died from morphine poisoning. The family doctor, who had issued death certificates for all the members of the family as having died of natural causes, was frankly annoyed. 'How can she have died of morphine poisoning?' he demanded at the inquest. 'When a person dies of morphine poisoning, the pupils of the eyes contract to pin-points. This is a diagnostic feature which is invariably present in cases of morphine poisoning. The pupils of the eyes of the deceased were perfectly normal.' The coroner was forced to admit that the doctor was perfectly correct.

Police had been informed of Captain Gibbs's suspicions regarding Nurse Toppan, and a detective was sent to question her in another town, Lowell, where she had moved to her new appointment after the deaths of the Davis family. The detective found that she was no longer there; the patient she had been looking after had died, and she had moved to Amherst. There she was apprehended. 'I have a clear conscience,' she said. 'I wouldn't kill a chicken.' Nevertheless she was charged with murder, and while she was in jail pending the forthcoming trial, many families campaigned for her and subscribed to a substantial fund for her defence.

Graves throughout the state of Massachusetts were being opened and bodies exhumed, and at every autopsy without exception the bodies were found to contain morphine. A pharmacist was found who had been supplying Nurse Toppan with the drug which she had obtained using forged doctors' prescriptions.

Eventually, Jane Toppan decided to make a full confession, and shocked the prison authorities by naming thirty-one persons whom she had poisoned. Her technique, she explained, was to mix morphine with atropine; the latter drug counteracts the effect of the morphine on the pupils of the eyes, so that they remain normal. Sometimes, she said, she fed the unfortunate patients with the mixture 'straight' as medicine, and at other times she had blended it into their food such as soup or gruel. She was able to accelerate or delay death at will by increasing or decreasing the amount of the deadly mixture she gave them.

At this point, perhaps, would be a good time to mention the reason why Jane Toppan had embarked upon her career of poisoning as many of her patients as she could. She did not do this for gain, as so many poisoners have done, forging wills, appropriating property after death, or drugging patients so that they did not know what they were doing when they signed papers. No: although some of her patients were comfortably off, even wealthy, she was not interested in their money or possessions. Jane Toppan killed solely for kicks.

'Everybody trusted me,' she is on record as saying. 'It was so easy. I felt strange when I watched them die. I was all excited and my blood seemed to sweep madly through my veins. It was the only pleasure I had ... I had to do it. They hadn't done anything to me and I gained nothing from their deaths except the excitement of watching them die. I couldn't resist doing it ... This was my ambition: to have killed more helpless people than any man or woman has ever killed.'

It is apparent that the 'excitement' Jane Toppan felt upon seeing her patients die, and 'the only pleasure she had' were a form of sexual excitement, and it is quite possible that she attained orgasm in this strange and terrible way, even though she may have been unaware that this was what was happening to her. In those days, of course, such matters as orgasm were not discussed openly, or read about in papers, magazines and books, as they are today. But although Jane Toppan might not have had any technical knowledge on this point, she could feel the thrill of physical sexual fulfilment just the same, albeit only in this bizarre fashion, and at the cost of the lives of the men and women entrusted to her care.

The trial struck horror into those who attended it, and many of Nurse Toppan's erstwhile supporters could not believe that her confession was really true. Several of the families of patients who had been her victims had refused to allow their bodies to be exhumed, so she was charged with a specimen eleven murders, although she had in fact given names and details of thirty-one. A plea of not guilty by reason of insanity was agreed between the defence and the prosecution, on condition that Jane Toppan would never be eligible for parole.

In June 1902 the nurse everyone had trusted was sent to the State Mental Institution at Taunton, Massachusetts, where she lingered for another thirty-six years without devising any opportunity of poisoning her fellow-inmates. She died in 1938 at the age of eighty-one. As we have seen, she had once told a woman friend that a lot of old people over eighty didn't want to live anyway, but she never put on record whether that applied to herself too.

11

Sweet Fanny Adams

Alton is midway between Farnham and Winchester, and is only two miles from the home of Jane Austen. A hundred and twenty years ago it was a much smaller town than it is now – little more than a large village nestling in the peaceful Hampshire countryside. And blackberry-picking was a more popular pastime in those days than it seems to be now: whole families would go out into the woods and the fields armed with baskets, and raid the hedges for Nature's bounty, not only blackberries but other fruits in their season – rose-hips, sloes and so on – which they would bring home rejoicing. Besides having provided the family with a pleasant afternoon in the fresh air – including, possibly, a picnic – the fruits of the hedgerow, in the hands of the womenfolk, would soon be turned into delicious jams and jellies, rose-hip syrup, blackberry and apple pies, and wines, of which elderberry was a favourite.

On the afternoon of 24 August 1867, however, it was not a family picnic party that went blackberrying but a little group of three friends. Two sisters, eight-year-old Fanny Adams and seven-year-old Eliza – known as Lizzie – were accompanied by their school classmate Minnie Warner, who was also eight. Each of the children had a large basket, and their destination was a field known as Flood Meadow, which was about four hundred yards from their adjoining homes in Tan House Lane, Alton. Flood Meadow was bordered by hedges rich in wild plants, blackberries in particular, and their parents had given them permission to stay out picking them until four o'clock, when they had to be home for their tea. Their mothers hoped they would not waste too much time playing about but fill their baskets to the brim. The mothers had high hopes of a bumper pie-making session, adding the berries to the apples grown in their own orchards.

The girls were hard at work blackberrying when a respectable-looking young man approached them. According to the later testimony of Minnie Warner, he made a curious remark as he drew level to where they were standing: 'Ah, my little children! Here you are again!' It was curious, because none of them had ever seen him before. He gave Minnie a halfpenny – which in those days was worth a lot more than it is now – and told her to go with Lizzie and spend it. Minnie said a halfpenny was not enough for the two of them to spend, and the friendly stranger gave her a penny to put with it. Clutching the three-halfpence, she went off with Lizzie.

The young man then offered Fanny a halfpenny to go with him to a hollow in an old road which led to the nearby village of Shalden. Fanny took the halfpenny, but declined to accompany the stranger. He then pressed a further twopence into her hand and picked her up bodily, and carried her off. Soon afterwards Lizzie and Minnie returned from the village sweet shop, having spent their three-halfpence, and looked for Fanny, who was nowhere to be found. They wandered around looking for her for some time, but gave up after a time and went home.

By now it was past four o'clock, and the parents of the children were wondering where they had got to. At about a quarter past four Lizzie and Minnie arrived home and told their parents that Fanny had disappeared and that they had last seen her with a strange young man who had helped them pick blackberries and then offered them money for sweets. The missing child's mother was very alarmed, since Fanny was not the kind of child who would wilfully disobey her parents by staying out later than she had been told. Mrs Adams rounded up all the neighbours who were available and went out to search for Fanny.

When they reached Flood Meadow, a young man appeared on the scene at about 5.30. Minnie immediately recognized him as the young man they had spoken to earlier. A Mrs Gardiner, one of the neighbours in the search party, happened to know him by sight, and challenged him. He was Frederick Baker, a twenty-nine-year-old solicitor's clerk. He admitted talking to the children and giving them money for sweets, but said that Fanny had left him later to rejoin her friends. His general air of respectability was such that Mrs

Gardiner, after saying, 'I have a good mind to give you in charge of the police!' did nothing further about the matter, convinced that her suspicions were unfounded. After all, although it was somewhat unusual for a complete stranger to give money to little children, it did not automatically follow that his intentions were reprehensible ... After all, the village folk were usually friendly, and he had first offered to help the children with their blackberrying.

Frederick Baker then joined a colleague from his office for a drink in the Swan Inn, Alton. He told this colleague, who was leaving the area the following day to take up another job, that he might join him.

The two men were still sitting in the pub discussing job prospects over their beer, when horror swept over the little town. At about seven o'clock a labourer walking through a hop field adjoining Flood Meadow stumbled into a pool of blood, and a moment later came upon the severed head of a child, which had been laid across two poles, in some kind of ritual fashion. The right ear had been cut off, and both eyes gouged out. Close by lay a leg, severed into a thigh and a lower leg and foot, and a little further on lay the dismembered torso. This had been cut open and nearly all the internal organs removed. Five incisions had been made in the liver; the entire contents of the chest cavity and of the pelvic area were missing.

The labourer was a rough-and-ready sort of fellow, but this was too much for him; he was violently sick. Afterwards, still trembling, he went to fetch a wheelbarrow and took the dreadful remains to the police. They immediately mounted a search for the remaining parts of the body, but were able to find only an arm and the heart. Finally, as a ghastly climax to their search, the two missing eyes were found floating in the River Wey, close to the bridge.

Frederick Baker was quickly taken into custody as the last person known to have been seen with the child. Despite blood being found on his clothing and the fact that he had two knives, one of them bloodstained, in his possession, he continued to deny all knowledge of the crime, maintaining stoutly that the girl had left him after a while to rejoin her companions. He was detained, pending further inquiries, as a prime suspect.

In the meantime, the remains had been placed in a sheet

and taken to the Leather Bottle public house in Amery Street. The coroner's inquest was held at another pub, the Duke's Head. Dr L. Leslie said that the dismembering of the body had been so complete that it was quite impossible to state whether the child had been criminally assaulted.

It appeared that on the day of the murder Frederick Baker had left the solicitors' office in Alton where he was employed at about 1.10 p.m., and had returned at 3.25 p.m. He had then gone out again at about 4.30, returning to the office once more at 5.50. Eyewitnesses were found who were able to place him near the scene of the crime at various material times. A married woman from the village who knew him had seen him talking to the children. At about two o'clock he was seen standing beside a gate near the fields, and at 3 o'clock another witness saw him in a field near the place where the body was subsequently found.

On his return to the office in the later part of the afternoon, a fellow-clerk said that 'he seemed to be disturbed and anxious' and that he had initiated a conversation about the child being missing. He was remembered to have made a curious remark: 'If the child is found murdered, the police are sure to blame me, as I was seen talking to her.' Later, in conversation with the colleague with whom he subsequently went for a drink in the Swan Inn, he made another remarkable statement, also remembered by others in the office. The talk had been about job prospects outside the Alton district. Baker had said he might be interested in leaving on the following day to look for a new job to start the next Monday. His friend had reminded him that he might not be able to get another job as a solicitor's clerk so soon, whereupon he replied, 'Oh, I could go as a butcher.'

After his arrest police visited his office, and in his desk they found his diary, in which he had written, under the date of 24 August 1867, 'Killed a young girl. It was fine and hot'. Asked at his subsequent trial about this diary entry, he replied that it merely meant that 'a young girl had been killed on a fine hot day'. He admitted that the handwriting was his, and to the ownership of the diary. Asked how he knew that the child had been killed before the news had reached the papers, he said that he had made the entry after Mrs Gardiner had spoken to him, adding that he was drunk at the time.

The remains of Fanny Adams were interred in Alton Cemetery on 28 August. Despite the burial service being conducted on a working day afternoon, a large number of people assembled. The Revd. W. Wilkins, curate of Thedden, pointed out during his address that this was the first murder to have been committed in Alton during the living memory of even the oldest of those present.

Baker appeared before a full bench of magistrates on the following day, 29 August 1867, at the Town Hall, and was committed for trial at Winchester Assizes which opened at the Castle on 5 December 1867. Baker, who pleaded not guilty, was defended by Mr Carter, and the judge was Mr Justice Mellor. Baker declared his innocence, stating that he had no motive, and pointing out that the two knives he had were far too small to have been capable of inflicting such frightful mutilations. In this he was supported by a medical witness, who said that, in his opinion, the bloodstained knife which had been found on the prisoner was not large or strong enough to have dismembered a human body. Yet no other weapon was produced, although the body had been cut into twenty pieces. The cause of death, according to the forensic evidence, was a blow to the head with a heavy stone.

Baker was next asked to state his reaction to having been positively identified by Minnie Warner as the man who had spoken to her and her friends. He said that an identification of a person by a child as young as Minnie Warner, who was only eight years of age, was 'too unreliable for any weight to be attached to it'.

The murder, according to forensic evidence, was committed some time between 1.40 and 3.30 p.m. on the afternoon of 24 August. Asked to account for the presence of blood on his sleeves, he gave the explanation which has so often been put forward in murder trials both before and since: 'I had a nosebleed'. Asked to explain why his boots, socks and the lower legs of his trousers were found to be wet when he was apprehended, as though he had attempted to wash them, he stated, 'I always walk through puddles when I go out for a walk.' The prosecution was quick to comment that such a statement was manifestly absurd. Baker was then asked why he had given money to the children, which he did not deny doing. He said that he often gave coins to children he might encounter while out on a walk, and thought nothing of it. It was not a crime, he pointed out, to talk to or give coppers to small children.

During the course of the trial, it was revealed that up to the age of twenty-six he had never touched alcohol. It was also pointed out that he was a regular churchgoer, and that every Sunday Baker would meticulously record his church attendances in the same diary which had been referred to earlier in the trial. Under cross-examination he revealed that he had been very distressed recently over a broken engagement and was suffering from depression, and he had also complained that his work was too much for him. Colleagues testified that he would on occasions burst into tears while sitting at his desk in the office.

His doctor testified that he did indeed suffer from frequent nosebleeds as well as severe head pains, and that there was a family history of insanity. He gave evidence that Baker had difficulty in controlling his emotions and in making and maintaining relationships with friends of either sex, especially with women. His broken engagement was a direct result of this difficulty. He was too unstable and insecure to enter into a firm commitment to another person such as that entailed by marriage. He also found it difficult to settle in and keep a job, the demands of work apparently being a source of stress which manifested itself in both mental and physical symptoms.

All this, however, failed to save Frederick Baker from the consequences of his actions. As Mr Justice Mellor pointed out in his summing-up, if it was not proved to the satisfaction of the jury that the prisoner was the murderer of Fanny Adams he should be acquitted, without taking into consideration the latent homicidal mania which was alleged to be rife in his family background. If the jury believed that he was not responsible for his actions then they should find for a verdict of insanity – again without reference to any family history. It was, after all, the judge continued, the accused who was on trial for murder, not his family. If the jury decided that the prisoner *was* responsible for his actions, then the only possible verdict was guilty as charged.

The jury retired, and were out for only a quarter of an hour before returning a unanimous verdict of guilty of murder. The image in their minds of that terrible hacking frenzy under a blazing August sun in the secluded hop field blotted out any possible arguments in mitigation.

Frederick Baker was executed on Christmas Eve 1867, in the presence of 5,000 people. He was one of the last men to be publicly hanged in front of the County Jail at Winchester.

Fanny's gravestone, which can still be seen in the cemetery at Alton, was erected by public subscription. It is inscribed as follows:

> Sacred to the memory of Fanny Adams, aged 8 years and 4 months, who was cruelly murdered on Saturday, August 24th, 1867.
>
> 'Fear not them which kill the body, but are not able to kill the soul, but rather fear him which is able to destroy both body and soul in hell.'

12

One Murder – Three Trials

Patrick Henry was a familiar figure in Boyle, Co. Roscommon, as he trudged about the town in his shabby overcoat, ragged trousers and down-at-heel shoes. 'Old Pat' as he was known, was sixty-seven years old, an unemployed man who drew six shillings a week dole and lived in a one-up, one-down hovel on the outskirts of town, apparently alone in the world, for he never had any visitors, nor did he ever visit anyone. But he was well known by sight to many of the local working folk, and so his sudden disappearance from the Boyle scene could not fail to be noted. One day he was shuffling through the streets as usual; the next day there was no sign of him, nor on any of the days after that. It was as though he had vanished into thin air. Just like that.

The front door of Old Pat's cottage had neither handle nor lock but was secured on the outside with a hasp and padlock when he was out and by bolts on the inside when he was at home. As he was out and about in the town during the day, the padlock was a common sight. Pat had always paid his two shillings weekly rent regularly, but on Saturday, 7 September 1935, he failed to pay for the first time. His landlady, a Miss Bridie O'Callaghan, who lived in another part of the town, at first ignored the default, but after a few weeks she called at the cottage and, finding it padlocked, assumed that Old Pat was out. She returned a few times during the following weeks, but the cottage was always locked. Then it suddenly struck her that she had not seen the old man about in the town for a long time. She used to see him several times a week as he passed her house on his jaunts into town. She thought back carefully and remembered seeing him on the Monday after the date his first default in the payment of his rent had been noted in her books. That would be Monday, 9 September.

Finally, on 13 December she thought he had been missing long enough. If he would not pay his rent, then she would find another tenant who would. So she went to the Gardaí and told them that her tenant had not been seen for more than three months, never mind paid his rent. Two Gardaí were detailed to go with her to visit the cottage, where they forced the padlock and opened the door.

Miss O'Callaghan followed them inside, but on seeing the body of a dead man lying on the floor in a state of advanced decomposition she rushed outside screaming. The dead man was her tenant, Patrick Henry.

He lay partly in the fireplace and partly on the floor, and had been savagely beaten to death. His skull had been fractured in several places by one tremendous blow with a blunt instrument. His jaw was broken, other facial bones were broken, and both the body and the clothing were very badly burned in places, many of the burns having preceded death, perhaps hastening it. The state pathologist who examined the body thought that Old Pat had been dead for two or three months.

The state of the room was horrifying, with dark, dried bloodstains everywhere: on the floor, under the bed, on the walls, on a bucket, on a hammer, and even on some of the sods of turf stacked by the fireplace for fuel. The cottage itself was as squalid a hovel as could be found in Boyle; it had no running water or sanitation, or electricity. The uncarpeted earth floor supported the barest minimum of furniture: two broken-down beds with makeshift bedding, a rickety deal table, two equally rickety kitchen chairs, and some battered iron cooking-pots on the fireplace, which burned only peat. The place was grimy beyond all imagining.

The first thing that struck the Gardaí was: how had Patrick Henry's murderer been able to enter the cottage to commit this crime? The interior of the house was as secure as it could be; quite apart from the padlocked front door, the back door was closed securely by a stout timber beam. No windows were open or broken, and the window-ledges and articles on them were thick with dust and obviously had not been disturbed for months. The last person to enter and leave the cottage – and therefore, it would seem, the murderer – had entered and left by the front door, and padlocked it behind him. So it would appear that he must have had a key.

Someone with a key? Could Old Pat have taken in a lodger?

Miss O'Callaghan was able to inform the Gardaí that she was aware that Pat had indeed taken in a lodger, although she did not know his name and had never seen him. She thought that this had been in about May 1935. The Gardaí now made inquiries of other townsfolk who had known Patrick Henry, and quickly discovered the identity of the lodger who, suspiciously enough, had disappeared from the Boyle scene at about the same time as Old Pat himself.

This man was Thomas Kelly, who had paid half of Henry's two shillings a week rent, and during the summer months worked with him cutting turf on and off, interspersed with drawing the dole when there was no turf-cutting work to be had. Kelly was fifty-six and had been born in a hamlet near Boyle, although he had spent most of his life as a nomad, working in various jobs for short periods to support himself as he travelled around, sometimes using the name Mooney. His usual practice was to work until he had saved enough to enable him to afford to live for some time without working. He had spent several years in America, where he had worked in various jobs and saved a sum equivalent to £1,300, a substantial amount at that time for a labouring man. Then he had decided to return to Ireland.

By 1934 he had not worked for four years and his funds were running low. He decided to return to Boyle, and in May 1935 went to live in the cottage of Patrick Henry. Obviously he must have had a key to the dwelling they shared. Now he had disappeared without trace, but the Gardaí were not to be discouraged, even if they were temporarily baffled.

The linings of Henry's jacket and waistcoat had been cut open in an apparent search for concealed money. His gold watch was missing, and there were no valuables or cash in the house. It had been widely rumoured that the old man had been carrying a wallet containing thirty to forty pounds in banknotes; others had averred that Old Pat had owned a small farm outside Boyle, which he had sold earlier that year, but these rumours had no basis in fact, though it certainly looked as if the killer had been influenced by them.

The precise date of Henry's death was, of course, uncertain, but a few clues pointed to an approximate estimate. Miss O'Callaghan had seen him on 9 September;

others were found who had seen him on 10 September. His unemployment money, due to be collected on 11 September for the week ending 10 September and which he had always collected regularly, was still lying unclaimed at the labour exchange. Kelly, too, had failed to draw his own dole money. It looked, on the face of things, as though Kelly had decamped on 10 September after murdering his companion, but against this was the theory that if Kelly had intended to kill and rob Henry he would have been more likely to do so after both he and his victim had collected their dole money. However, all this was sheer conjecture, for there was no proof at all that Kelly had murdered Henry or even that he had been the last person to see him alive. The Gardaí would need a great deal more than these slender clues to go on, but despite exhaustive inquiries, including liaison with the English police and newspaper and radio appeals, there was no news of him, and it was another five months before the Gardaí made any further progress.

On 21 May 1936 the Hibernian Bank in Sligo, where Kelly had a small deposit account, received a deposit receipt from a bank in Coatbridge, near Glasgow, for collection. The Sligo bank returned it to the Scottish bank, to be represented after ten days, i.e. on 31 May, and at the same time informed the Gardaí.

On 22 May a party of Gardaí left Dublin for Glasgow. Two of the party knew Kelly by sight, and they, assisted by Scottish police officers, began their surveillance of the Coatbridge branch of the bank, watching from premises situated opposite. It was a tedious business watching the building day after day and the many customers going in and out of the bank, but after thirteen days the silent watchers had their reward. On 5 June, at 2.30 p.m., Kelly appeared in the street, sporting a moustache and spectacles which he had never worn in Boyle, and entered the bank. Garda Robert Shaw from Boyle and Constable Graham Young of the Scottish police, both in plain clothes, crossed the street, and when Kelly came out of the bank they followed him for a short distance. Young then caught up with Kelly and asked him his name, to which he replied, 'John Hill.' Asked where he lived, he said, 'Coatbridge.' Shaw then joined his colleague and asked Kelly to accompany them to the police station. Shaw then said, 'You're Tom Kelly. Don't you remember me?' Kelly grudgingly admitted that he did. The three men then walked to the police station nearby.

At the entrance Young went in first, followed by Kelly. While Young was ahead, Kelly quickly pulled his hand from his trousers' pocket and, wielding a cut-throat razor, slashed the left side of his neck. The two officers grabbed him, managed to wrest the blade from him, miraculously without getting cut themselves, and tried to overpower him, but despite Kelly's considerable seniority in age he was almost too strong for them and they had to summon the help of four more police officers before he could be subdued. First aid was applied to the wound, but even that Kelly resisted, and his fierce struggles had to be forcibly overcome before a doctor could stitch the wound. Kelly had only just missed severing his carotid artery by less than an inch. Kelly was then taken to a Glasgow hospital where he was kept under police guard until he was sufficiently recovered to be returned to Ireland, under heavy guard, to stand trial for murder. He was charged with having murdered Patrick Henry, to which he made no reply.

The trial opened on 10 November 1936, presided over by Mr Justice O'Byrne, KC. Prosecuting were Mr Martin Maguire and Mr Kevin Haugh; for the defence were Mr Ralph Brereton-Barry, KC and Mr Robert Hogan. The date alleged for the crime being 11 September 1935, the vital question was: when had Patrick Henry last been seen alive?

Miss Bridie O'Callaghan repeated in the witness-box what she had told the Gardaí, that she had last seen Henry on 9 September. Thomas Mayne, a cattle-dealer who lived two doors from Henry, said that he saw him on 10 September, which was the day of the Boyle Fair, but when cross-examined by Mr Brereton-Barry he said that on 11 September Henry 'could have been outside his cottage' although 'he was quite sure he had no recollection of seeing him there'. Yet at the preliminary inquiry in the district court he had sworn: 'I last saw Henry on the evening of 10 or 11 September: I cannot remember which. I saw him outside his house between 6 and 7 p.m.' Asked to say whether he was now quite sure that he could not remember which was the date, he said that 'it was very hard to remember, but he thought it might have been the Tuesday' (10 September). With witnesses giving evidence as confused as this one, the first seeds of doubt had been sown ....

A Mrs Brennan, who lived in the cottage adjoining Henry's, spoke of his regular habit of going out every morning for his newspaper, and she was quite definite that she had also seen him on 10 September entering his cottage between 7 and 8 p.m., after which she never saw him again. She last saw Kelly on the Wednesday, 11 September, going into the cottage between 1 and 2 p.m., coming out again ten or fifteen minutes later, wearing an overcoat over a brown suit. He was not carrying a suitcase. When he had come to live there he had brought two suitcases.

The wall which divided her cottage from her neighbours' was not thick enough to prevent her from hearing some sounds, such as voices and the setting and lighting of the fire every morning between 8 and 9 a.m. On 11 September, she testified, she heard these latter sounds between 7 and 8 a.m. – earlier than ever before. She particularly remembered the date because the court was sitting in the town that day. There had been silence, she continued, from Henry's cottage between Tuesday evening and Wednesday morning – a small point in favour of the defence, who contended (though not very convincingly) that the murder must have been a noisy and violent affair. Why should it have been, if Henry had been felled by the first blow?

The prosecution was able to show that all had not been well between Henry and his lodger. In August 1935, as Kelly and an acquaintance named John O'Connor were chatting in the street, Henry passed by and he and Kelly looked away from one another. 'Are you not talking to him?' asked O'Connor. 'No one would want to talk to that contrary old bastard!' said Kelly angrily.

A week later, O'Connor said, the two men again cut each other dead in the street, and on 10 September, as Kelly was talking to one James Lynch, Henry came out of the labour exchange and crossed the street to avoid them, upon which Lynch drew Kelly's attention to him. 'I will do that old bugger in one of these days!' exclaimed Kelly viciously. Yet neither Mrs Brennan, nor Henry's other immediate neighbour McLachlan, had ever heard them quarrelling. Lynch used to see Henry regularly at the labour exchange, but he had seen neither Henry nor Kelly since 10 September, a date he remembered because a travelling circus had visited Boyle that day.

Charles McCormack gave the same date for seeing Kelly last, though with less certainty ('in or about 10 September, about two nights before the Boyle Show' (which had been held on 12 September). He had seen Kelly at the Diamond, a working men's club in Boyle where he often met Kelly, who used to play a card-game called nap and generally was in the club from about 7 to 11 p.m. Another man named Reynolds testified that he had seen Kelly in the club the same night, and confirmed that it was definitely on 10 September. The next day (11 September) Reynolds attended the labour exchange, but neither Henry nor Kelly turned up that day, nor did he ever see either of them again. The manager of the labour exchange confirmed that each man had six shillings due to him to be collected; both, he said, had attended on the previous day to sign on.

The prosecution now rested their case, and Mr Maguire asked for leave to amend the alleged murder date from that charged (11 September) to 10 September. Mr Brereton-Barry raised no objection and the amendment was allowed.

Kelly now went into the witness-box. He said that he had been at the fair in Boyle on 10 September, met friends from Longford with whom he had some drinks, and went to the Diamond Club that evening, as McCormack and Reynolds had testified earlier. He said that he had left Henry alive and well at home. When the club closed Kelly went home. Henry was then in bed, and he (Kelly) went to bed himself.

The next morning at 8.30 he awoke, feeling the after-effects of the previous night's boozing. He made up the fire in the kitchen, then he and Henry ate breakfast together and talked about the forthcoming Show. After breakfast Henry went out, and Kelly left at about 10.30 to fetch bread. On the way he met Henry returning home, and spoke to him. He stayed in town until about one o'clock. When he returned to the cottage he found Henry reading the daily paper.

Kelly said that he left Boyle on 11 September and, after first going to Sligo to make a withdrawal of £10 from his bank, took an early train to Belfast. He had, he said, £53 in cash on him when he left Boyle, and with the £63 he now had, he spent a week in Belfast before leaving for Glasgow. In Coatbridge he obtained casual work looking after cattle at five shillings per day.

Mr Hogan now asked him: 'Is there any truth in the

suggestion that you killed Patrick Henry?' to which Kelly replied, 'I never had anything to do with it.'

Asked why he had left his suitcase in Henry's cottage, he said that he had no spare clothes to put in it, as his blue suit was worn out and there was no sense in taking an empty suitcase with him. It was pointed out to him that the trousers of his blue suit were missing, though the jacket had been left hanging in the cottage, but he could not explain what had happened to them, and the suggestion was that the trousers had been burnt or otherwise destroyed because of incriminating bloodstains.

Mr Maguire handed Kelly two pairs of trousers which had been found in the cottage, and asked him whether either pair was his. Kelly hesitated, and remained silent.

'If you have any doubt about them, I will ask you to put them on,' Mr Maguire persisted.

Kelly replied, 'I have a pair like them.'

Asked why he had not collected his unemployment money on the morning when he left Boyle, Kelly replied, 'I was going away and I did not think of it.' This was only one of the lame excuses he came up with to various questions in his cross-examination. Asked whether he could suggest why Henry had also not collected his dole money, Kelly replied, 'I don't know. What Pat did was nothing to do with me.' Kelly denied cutting open Henry's garments to look for hidden money. He also denied that he and Henry had ever fallen out, or that he had ever referred to him in scathing terms, or threatened to kill him. 'That's all a pack of lies!' he said heatedly. 'The two of us were on friendly terms.'

By the time the evidence for the defence had closed and Counsels' speeches had ended, it was 7.30 p.m. and the jury were sequestered for another night. The next morning the judge began his charge to the jury. Mr Justice O'Byrne was a judge of distinction – conscientious, principled, a sound lawyer and a man of balanced mind. The motive for the crime, according to the prosecution's theory, was gain. This was inconsistent with the prosecution's own evidence that the two men had been on bad terms and that murder could have followed an angry but unpremeditated quarrel. As the defence pointed out, if gain were the motive then Kelly's withdrawal of £10 from the Sligo bank was not only pointless but indeed dangerous if he were a fugitive from justice and therefore pressed for time, and if he were attempting to flee it is incomprehensible that he would have left £80 in his bank account as he did.

The judge dealt adequately with these points, but when he came to the defence argument that anybody had the same opportunity of committing the crime that Kelly had had, he said: 'You have only to consider for a moment that this cannot be so ...,' going on to describe the lonely domestic life of the two men, whose threshold no visitor ever crossed, and asked: 'Who had such an opportunity for committing the crime as the accused? – the man who was living in the same house, the man who could go into or out of the house without arousing suspicion, the man who could get into the position to deliver such a crushing blow without arousing any suspicion on the part of his victim ....'

As to the controversial date of Henry's death, the judge correctly pointed out that if he had been alive on 12 September one would have expected him to be seen by Mrs Brennan, even though she did not see him every day, and that he would have in any case collected his dole money.

The jury retired at 1.25 p.m. and took just two hours to find Kelly guilty of murder. When the judge asked Kelly whether he had anything to say why sentence should not be pronounced according to law, he answered, 'Nothing, my lord.' Judge O'Byrne then sentenced him to be executed on 3 December 1936, saying that he entirely agreed with the jury's verdict, and appealed to Kelly to use the short time left to him in this life to make his peace with his Creator, 'the Great Judge before Whom we shall all have to appear one day'.

The trial had taken four days, ending on 14 November. Kelly was only nineteen days away from death. He appealed on various grounds, but four days after the trial his solicitor, Mr Christopher Callum of Boyle, was told by three fellow-citizens, Edward Farrell, John Tuite and Thomas Johnston, that each had read about the trial and could prove that Henry was alive on 12 September 1935. Others, too, came forward with the same information, and by 27 November the total was seven persons, none of whom had been known to Mr Callum before the trial. So the Court of Criminal Appeal was asked, for the first time since its formation, to allow the appeal on the additional grounds that these seven witnesses could prove that Henry was alive on

12 September 1935 and that a new trial should be directed so that another jury could hear their evidence. The Court directed the attendance of the seven before them, and when they had been heard the Court quashed the conviction and ordered a new trial, but only on those grounds, rejecting any others. Thus Kelly's time in this world was extended considerably past 3 December, and his new trial was set for 15 April 1937 before Mr Justice Hanna.

The new defence witnesses were remarkably consistent, and gave realistic and convincing details. John Tuite stated that he saw Henry between 9.30 and 10 a.m. on the day of the Show (12 September), and John Ryan said he saw him soon after that time in the town. Edward Farrell said that he actually spoke to him at five minutes to eleven that morning, on the road leading to the Show. Asked why he could be so precise about the time, he replied that it was because it was just five minutes before he had an appointment to meet a friend at 11 o'clock who was going to the Show with him.

Robert Irwin stated that he saw Henry twice on 12 September, once in the morning when Henry was accompanied by others, and once in the afternoon when he was alone. Martin Forde said he met Henry on his (Forde's) way to the Show in the evening and exchanged greetings with him. A Mrs Kenny testified that she met him as she stood on a bridge. 'Not much of a crowd at the Show this year,' Henry had observed, after returning Mrs Kenny's 'Good-evening'.

These people could not all have made the same mistake as to the date on which they had seen Henry, especially since most of them did not even know Kelly, and the prosecution's suggestion of a conspiracy to commit perjury sounded too far-fetched to be true. As the judge pointed out to the jury, the various times and occasions referred to by the seven witnesses fitted together hour by hour right through the day like the pieces of a jigsaw puzzle, and if believed could provide the best possible alibi for the accused. The defence case was further strengthened when Dr Leyland, another defence witness, said that in his opinion Henry had not been dead as long as three months when his body was found, and Dr McGrath, the state pathologist, agreed that Henry had been dead for about two months. It would seem, then, that Kelly's departure from Boyle at the time when Henry was no longer seen around the town was mere coincidence.

So, by the time the jury retired, Kelly seemed to stand a good chance of acquittal. Two hours later the jury returned, and when the foreman rose to speak a deathly hush fell upon the court. All he said, however, was that the jury wished to hear the evidence of a man named Mulvaney who had not been called by the prosecution and who might be able to give important evidence.

Mulvaney was called to the box by the judge, and testified that he had seen Henry in Boyle on 12 September. But when Mr Maguire cross-examined him he elicited from him that he had told the Gardaí that he had not seen Henry, whom he knew well, on the day of the Show, and that a month later he called again at the police station and repeated his statement to the Superintendent. Thus was yet more confusion added to surround the critical date of 12 September ....

The jury again retired, and Kelly had to spend two more hours in suspense. Then the twelve reappeared, and once again that terrible silence reigned as the registrar stood to ask whether they had reached their verdict, and a man's life hung in the balance. 'No, my lord', said the foreman, 'we cannot agree upon a verdict.'

Kelly's feelings can be more easily conjectured than described as he was returned to the cells to await his third trial, which was delayed until 15 November 1937 and took six days, before Mr Justice Duffy.

So Kelly heard himself being charged with murder for the fifth time – once in the police station in Boyle, once in the district court at the preliminary hearing, and three times in the Central Criminal Court in Dublin.

All the evidence was now put forward again. The defence now had two more witnesses, Edward Flanagan, who stated that he had said 'Good-evening' to Henry as they met on the road from the Show on 12 September, and Edward Johnston, who testified that he had seen Henry on the same day standing at the corner of the Northern Bank building in Boyle. Johnston had told his own solicitor that he was 'almost sure' it was Henry, and was now asked in cross-examination whether he was still of that opinion. 'I am sure of it now', the witness replied, 'because I never saw Henry again since that day.'

The third jury had now heard eleven people, all of whom averred that they had seen Henry alive on 12 September.

Surely this must have been in Kelly's favour, but the judge reminded the jury that most of these witnesses did not even know Kelly, and any who did know him by sight were not friends of his. One must feel that at least one of these eleven should have been believed; if only one were to be believed, then that was the end of the case, and Kelly must be acquitted. One more disagreement would give Kelly a good chance that the prosecution would drop the case.

However, this time there was no disagreement, and Kelly was found guilty. For the second time he heard himself being sentenced to death, and for the second time he said nothing when asked whether he had anything to say.

The judge created a precedent by omitting to don the black cap as he sentenced the accused with the fatal words; whether this was by design or otherwise will never be known. Kelly appealed once more, but the appeal failed; but on 21 December 1937 the government commuted his sentence to penal servitude for life. Kelly was released just one week short of ten years later, on 17 December 1947. Nothing seems to be known about what happened to him after this.

One may wonder why the third jury did not have the same doubts which some of the second jury must have had. Could one really be certain that every one of those eleven witnesses was wrong?

13

Murder in the Close

At one-thirty in the afternoon of Friday, 20 April 1934, a little girl of eight, Helen Priestly, was sent by her mother to the local Co-op to buy a loaf of bread. The shop was less than a hundred yards from the child's home, so she was expected back in less than ten minutes. She had to be back at school by two o'clock.

When Helen had not returned home by ten to two, Mrs Priestly started to worry; it was most unlike Helen to dally when school time was approaching. Helen enjoyed school and hated to be late, even if she had a valid reason. She would have had to return home first not only to bring the bread but also to pick up her schoolbag of books and pencils, which she would need for the afternoon's lessons.

Mrs Priestly went to the window of their ground floor flat and looked out along the street, which was situated in a working-class district of Aberdeen. There was no sign of the child, so she asked her nearest neighbours whether they had seen her; no one had. She then went to the Co-op, where she was told that Helen, whom the assistants knew well, had bought the bread and had then left the shop with the loaf under her arm and the till receipt in her pocket.

After returning home to see whether Helen had returned in her absence, Mrs Priestly went to the school, which was only three minutes' walk away. It was just two o'clock, and the children were going in. Spotting a classmate of Helen's, who was the child of a neighbour, Mrs Priestly asked her to look inside the school to see whether Helen was there. She was not.

Returning home, Mrs Priestly was by now thoroughly alarmed. Helen would never have played truant, or gone to a friend's home without asking permission. Mrs Priestly made a final search of her home, looking in cupboards and wardrobes, and even checking that she had not locked herself in the outside loo or in the washhouse in the yard, both of which were shared by the tenants of all the four ground floor flats, which were called tenements. The building was divided into blocks called closes, each of which contained four tenements on every floor, and each close had several floors.

There was no sign of the missing child, so Mrs Priestly decided to go and inform her husband, who was at work. Mr Priestly, who was a painter and decorator, left his work and together with his wife went to the police to report Helen missing. Police immediately instituted a search, which was joined by groups of the missing child's neighbours.

Rain started to fall heavily at about eight o'clock, which hampered the searchers, but most of them continued during that wet and windy night until twelve o'clock. Helen's father was driven around the area in a friend's car, while his wife called on all the people she knew in the neighbourhood, except one woman in the close with whom she was not on speaking terms. Apparently there was some kind of a feud between the two families, and when the police were making their house-to-house inquiries they discovered that this woman and her husband, Alexander and Jeannie Donald, who had a nine-year-old daughter who attended the same school as Helen Priestly, were the only ones among the Priestly family's neighbours who did not go out and join the search for the missing child. When asked why they did not go, the woman said, 'Aw, what guid would it do?' and her husband added, 'She's right – they hae dozens o' folks oot lookin' alrreidy. Besides. I dinna want tae join all them screechin' women.'

At midnight the search-parties called a halt, likewise the police, who had examined every nook and cranny in the close and its immediate vicinity. The search would be resumed at first light the following morning.

At five o'clock Andrew Birnie was coming home from the night shift at his factory job. To reach his tenement, which was on one of the upper floors in the same close as the Priestly family, he had to enter a passage between the two rear tenements on the ground floor, with the doors to the outside lavatory and washhouse on either side, in order to reach the stairs. Between two of these rear doors was a small alcove or recess, and as Birnie passed this he noticed a sack lying on the ground against the wall. Taking a closer look, he saw a child's shod and stockinged foot protruding from the sack. He went straight to the police.

There was a great deal of shouting and screaming and banging of doors, and then a police car arrived. Dr Richards, the city police surgeon, who was also a lecturer in forensic medicine at Aberdeen University, examined the body on the spot, which proved to be that of the missing child. She was fully-clothed except for her knickers and her school beret. On her palm was an impression of the print from the till receipt she had been given on purchasing the bread, which she had evidently removed from her pocket (where the shop assistant had seen her put it) and carried in her hand so as to be sure not to lose it. There was no sign of this till receipt in the sack, or anywhere nearby. The sack contained several cinders, like those from a domestic boiler; some had got into her hair as she had been placed head first into the sack.

Vomit stains were apparent on her face and clothing, and the location of post-mortem lividity (the dark staining seen at the points where a dead body is lowest in position) showed that she had lain on her left side for several hours after death, although when found she was lying on her right side. The body was completely rigid, proving that she had been dead for twelve hours or more. Very serious internal injuries and blood on her thighs and lower regions pointed to the fact that she had been subjected to a savage sexual attack.

At five past seven the body was taken to the city mortuary for formal identification and a full autopsy by Dr Richards and Professor Shennan, Professor of Pathology at the University. While the results of this were awaited, the police now busied themselves with a more thorough and intensive search of the close where the body had been found. Various clues indicated to them that it was extremely unlikely that the crime had been committed anywhere else. The sack, a jute bag, had a depression at the child's waist level, as though the body, in its covering, had been carried over the arm, but it was not creased and wrinkled as it would have been if it had been carried any appreciable distance. Both the sack, the girl's body and the clothing were dry, despite the fact that it had been raining hard all night. There was a pool of water outside the rear entrance to the close, and the ground in the yard was soft, yet there were no footprints there, or muddy footprints in the passage. Members of the search-parties who had been walking near the tenements or standing about in the vicinity for most of the night were all questioned intensively, but no one reported seeing any suspicious person or anyone carrying a bundle or parcel of any kind, or hearing any unusual sounds.

There had been, in fact, a great deal of toing and froing during the night. The police had searched the backyard and all the coal bunkers, obtaining the keys from all the tenants, at eleven o'clock. The dead child's father had been in and out several times since midnight carrying on his search, and three of the other tenants had used the outside lavatory at 1.30, 4.30 and 4.40 a.m. respectively. There was no bundle on the floor between the doors in the rear passage up to that time.

The police were fairly certain that the murder had been committed by someone in the close, who had kept the body in the tenement for several hours and then nipped out to deposit it in the recess when the coast was clear. All the signs pointed to this being the case. The police now visited every tenement and questioned every male over sixteen. Every man who lived in those tenements was able to account for his movements on that dreadful night. Many worked a night-shift in local factories. The police were stymied; had an unknown intruder managed to sneak in after all, and hide in one of the tenements? How had he managed to hide the body for so long before depositing it in the alcove unseen? And how had he managed to escape the vigilance of half the population of the street as well as the police, in effecting his escape? The police thought the intruder theory was highly improbable.

Later that day the results of the full post-mortem examination were received. The child had been strangled. The condition of the stomach showed that death had occurred between one and two hours after her last meal, which was known to have been at 12.30, which put her death at between 1.30 and 2.30 p.m. Later, some further evidence narrowed this period to between 1.45 and 2 p.m.

The autopsy also showed that, while the rape injuries were very severe and had been inflicted before death, they were not characteristic of injuries that could have occurred in the process of penetration by a male. Firstly, no seminal fluid was found either in or on the body, or on the sack or the clothing; secondly, the more serious injuries, which had ruptured the perineum and the abdominal wall internally, had been made by a pointed or sharp instrument such as a poker. The possibility now had to be considered that the child had not been raped by a male at all but had been attacked by a woman, who had injured her in such a way as to simulate rape and thereby divert suspicion from herself.

Further evidence now came to light that Helen Priestly had been seen by a neighbour's child walking home with the bread at a quarter to two. Another neighbour stated that he heard what could have been a child's scream at about two o'clock from the direction of the close where the Priestly family lived. He was a roof-tiler who had been working on the roof of an adjoining close at the time, and said he had taken no notice, because 'kids scream all the time as they play in and around the closes'. No one else appeared to have heard any child scream at that time, and his evidence was not very favourably regarded at the subsequent trial. The roofer had not mentioned it to anyone at the time, even after learning that a child from that close had disappeared. He did not report it to the police until three days after the murder.

Two days after the finding of the body, the police, having visited all the other tenements in the murder close, were interviewing Alexander and Jeannie Donald, the only tenants who had not joined the search-party from their floor. A dour and taciturn couple, they kept themselves very much to themselves; they did not even allow their daughter to play with the children of other tenants out of school hours. Apparently the woman had quarrelled with Mrs Priestly in the past over an incident when their two respective daughters had come to blows, the argument having hinged on which child had hit the other first. While Mrs Priestly had stated that she had not been on speaking terms with Mrs Donald for about four years, Mrs Donald maintained that it was for only about a year.

Jeannie Donald, thirty-eight, was a regular churchgoer and a member of the local Mothers' Union meeting group which met regularly each week at the Salvation Army's headquarters. She was intensely and fiercely proud of her daughter, also named Jeannie like herself, who although only nine years of age had already gained several medals and certificates in various arts subjects at school. On the day of Helen Priestly's disappearance Mrs Donald spent more than two hours pressing and ironing her daughter's school-clothes and also some dresses for her school play rehearsal. When her daughter came home from school she had her tea with the family, and then she went to the rehearsal with her mother. Her father called for them after the rehearsal and escorted them home. Alexander Donald worked as a hairdresser, who came home for lunch, as also did the child, at midday every day.

All this information was freely given to the police. When asked to account for their movements on 20 April at around the time Helen was killed, Jeannie Donald said that she left the tenement at about ten or fifteen minutes past one to go to the weekly market, where she purchased eggs and oranges, and then went to a shop called Morrison's to buy some material for a new dress for her daughter, but found none suitable. She then went home, where she saw a number of the tenants standing about in the street outside. She did not ask anyone what was wrong, but went straight in and started the ironing, after putting away the eggs and oranges and putting her purse into the kitchen dresser drawer. A neighbour told her at about four o'clock that Helen was missing, to which she replied, 'That must be what everybody was all standing around for, I suppose.'

All this sounded very plausible, but the police were not satisfied. At 9 p.m. they asked the Donalds for permission to search their tenement, which they readily agreed to allow them to do. Some bloodstains, admittedly small ones, were found on certain articles in the flat. Mrs Donald's visit to the market also did not stand up to investigation. The prices she said she had paid for the eggs and oranges were not correct for the date in' question, but they were accurate for the previous Friday. Morrison's shop had also been closed that day. The inference was that Mrs Donald had described her visit to the market the previous week, when Morrison's had also been open.

Forensic evidence was also to play a large part. Materials found in the sack with the body included cinders from a kitchen boiler, household fluff and a few hairs. The dead child's knickers and her school beret were still missing, and were searched for in the Donalds' flat along with the till receipt from the Co-op, the loaf of bread, and the instrument used to inflict the injuries. Because of their nature, any bloodstains found on such an instrument might be contaminated with intestinal bacteria. The origin of the sack itself also might provide a useful clue.

While there were hundreds, perhaps thousands, of such sacks circulating in Aberdeen for the transport of potatoes and such items, this particular one bore black marks on the outside caused by the sooty bottoms of cooking-pots. This suggested that the sack had been kept on the floor of a kitchen and pots placed on it, or wiped on it when taken from the black range stove. There was also a hole in one corner, suggesting that it might at some time have been kept hanging on a hook. The police found nine more sacks similar to the murder sack in the Donalds' tenement, five of which had a hole in one corner and three of which bore black sooty pot-marks. Although this was suspicious, it was still not proof.

In the sack there was a quantity of washed cinders from a boiler. All the tenements in the close had a boiler, but Mrs Donald was the only one of the tenants who habitually washed and kept her cinders for reuse. Similar washed cinders were found in the Donalds' kitchen.

Hairs found in the sack were not those of the child but were found to be similar to those obtained from a hairbrush belonging to Mrs Donald. They showed an irregularity of contour, with many definite twists, caused by a particular kind of permanent waving. In the household dust and fluff found in the sack, more than 200 different components were identified, twenty-five of which were fibres identical to those found in the household fluff and dust collected from the Donalds' tenement. Household fluff was taken from all the other tenements in the close and investigated under the comparison microscope, but in no case could the forensic team find any similarities. The absolute matching of so many fibres seemed to be conclusive proof that those found in the sack had originated in the Donalds' home.

Not surprisingly, the more obvious clues sought were not to be found. Five days had elapsed since the crime, so there had been ample time to destroy the more incriminating evidence. The missing knickers and beret were never found, nor was the instrument used to inflict the dreadful injuries. Part of a loaf of bread was discovered, of the type bought by Helen Priestly, and not usually eaten by the Donalds. More incriminating, however, was the torn piece of a till receipt found in the fireplace. On one side was a green line identical with the green line on all Co-op till receipts, not used by other shops. There were also figures forming the date '20 Apl 1934' as used by the shop, though the portion bearing the price was missing.

Human blood was found on a number of articles in the tenement, including two newspapers dated 19 April, the day before the crime, two washcloths, a scrubbing-brush, a box of soap-flakes and some linoleum taken from the floor of a cupboard under the kitchen sink. The blood was Group O, the same group as that of the child. Mrs Donald's blood was found to be of a different group. At the subsequent trial the defence pointed out that because the blood was Group O this did not prove that it was the child's, since forty-two per cent of the white population have Group O blood.

The linoleum taken from under the sink showed a rectangular mark where a cinder-box had habitually stood, but this box had disappeared. The box would have been large enough to hide a small child's body, and it would seem that if this had been the case the box would have become bloodstained and was therefore subsequently destroyed. Like the missing knickers, beret and, possibly, some floorcloths and towels which were apparently also missing, the wooden box could have been dismantled and burnt to ashes in the boiler. The kitchen doorknob, the handle of the door of the cupboard under the sink, and parts of the linoleum on the kitchen floor all bore unmistakable evidence of having been recently washed. In all, no fewer than 253 exhibits were shown at the subsequent trial, all of which had been taken from the Donalds' home.

On 25 April, after the police had been in their tenement for thirteen hours, the Donalds were arrested and charged with the murder of Helen Priestly. Both denied the crime. They were taken from their home at 12.15 midnight in a police van, to the accompaniment of shrieks and catcalls from women neighbours and shouts and oaths from the men. On 11 June Alexander Donald was released, it having been proved that he was at work at the material time in his hairdresser's salon and had no knowledge of the crime.

Jeannie Donald, for all her vehement denials, was not so lucky. Her alibi was easily broken. Her trial took place on 16 July 1934, a jury of ten men and five women having been sworn in according to Scottish law. No fewer than 164 witnesses were called. During all this the accused woman remained silent and unmoved. Not once did she show any emotion, not even when her own daughter was called as a witness. Only when the death sentence was passed did her outward calm disintegrate.

The jury had been out for only eighteen minutes before returning a unanimous verdict of guilty. Then, and only then, did the woman collapse in the dock, and after sentence was carried down to the cells. At her trial the fifteen good Scots men and women were agreed as with one voice that Jeannie Donald must pay the penalty, but the death sentence was later commuted to penal servitude for life.

Jeannie Donald was released in 1944.

14

The Hi-fi Murders

Courtney Naisbitt was, like most sixteen-year-old high school students, a fun-loving boy – not the kind of fellow to sit at home and mope when he could be out and about in town with his friends. On 22 April 1974, after supper, his parents decided to go out, so he decided to go out, too. But first he would have to finish his English and maths homework to hand in on the following day. As well as being a fun-loving boy, he was also a conscientious one. Besides, if he wanted to succeed in his chosen career of engineering, he could not afford to neglect his studies.

At about eight o'clock he had completed his homework and then changed out of his school-clothes to go out and meet some of his friends. He knew that two of his best buddies, Stan Walker and Michelle Ansley, were looking after a hi-fi shop owned by a friend of theirs while he was away for the day. The shop was at 2323 Wessington Boulevard, in their home community of Ogden, Utah, and as Courtney made his way purposefully along the street he realized that it would soon be the store's closing time and he and his friends would be able to enjoy listening to records until the owner's return when Stan and Michelle would account to him for the takings to be banked the following day.

As Courtney arrived at the shop, all was quiet. Popping his head round the door, he called 'Hi!' to his friends, but no one answered. He entered the store and closed the door. He could not see Stan or Michelle, but guessed that they were down in the basement making coffee. Odd, though – leaving the door open when the store was unattended – very odd indeed. He decided to go and join them in the basement and give them a friendly reminder that it was not a good idea. Quickly he moved towards the basement and found himself joining his friends even more rapidly than he had anticipated, as he was grabbed from behind and bundled unceremoniously down the stairs. He had disturbed a robbery ....

Courtney was trussed hand and foot and forced to lie on the floor alongside his two friends, who had been similarly treated. Courtney observed that there were three intruders, all armed with various weapons, so he thought discretion the better part of valour and decided not to try to call for help. Besides, who would hear him from the depths of the basement? Someone would no doubt come along and find them later when the robbers had fled with their loot, and let them go. Life was of more value than property ....

Someone did come along – Carol Naisbitt, Courtney's mother, who was looking for him, and almost immediately afterwards Orren Walker, Stan's father, looking for his son. The robbers grabbed them both, tied them up just like the others, and within minutes five victims lay trussed like chickens in a row on the floor of the basement of the hi-fi shop.

The intruders seized wallets, jewellery, purses and rings from their captives, and wrenched off their wristwatches. The robbers, however, were in no hurry to flee with their ill-gotten gains. Instead, they embarked upon an orgy of unbelievably savage violence. Taking a bottle from a brown paper bag, one of the assailants waved it in front of the row of bound victims, declaring, 'It's a mixture of vodka and a German drug. We're going to have a little cocktail party!' He poured a thick blue liquid from the bottle into a cup and forced it down the throat of Stan Walker, who gagged and vomited as the liquid burned his mouth and throat, helpless to avoid it because of his bonds. His attacker then did the same thing with all four of the other victims, pausing only to refill the cup from the bottle.

The unfortunate captives had been forced to drink Drano, a caustic liquid used to unblock drains. The legend on the label read: 'Tough on clogs – won't hurt pipes!'

The intruders then systematically shot four of their captives in the back of the head, execution-style, after first rolling them over face down. First to be shot was Carol Naisbitt, then Courtney, then Stan, and then Orren Walker. Michelle Ansley, a nineteen-year-old blonde, was left until last. She was raped repeatedly by the ringleader of the robbers, then despatched with a bullet in the head and left lying naked beside the other victims. Finally, this man thrust a ballpoint pen into one of Orren Walker's ears and kicked it into his head until it protruded into his throat. The three then departed, pocketing about 300 dollars from the till and taking a large number of stereo recorders and other hi-fi equipment, and leaving their victims in the basement for dead.

Only three were in fact dead: Stan Walker, Michelle Ansley and Carol Naisbitt. Courtney Naisbitt and Orren Walker were still alive, but badly wounded.

When the Naisbitts had returned home after their night out, they were concerned that Courtney was not at home. It was most unlike the teenager to stay out late, especially since he had given them no indication that he would be home later than usual. Courtney's father first called all his son's known friends on the telephone to see if he was with any of them, and he was disturbed to be informed by Orren Walker's wife that their son had not come home either, and that her husband had just left to go and look for him. Mr Naisbitt then asked his wife Carol to take the car and see if she could see him anywhere around town, while he would stay by the telephone in case Courtney called to say he was in some kind of trouble and needed help. Perhaps he had been taken ill? Stan Walker was his best friend – perhaps Stan was looking after him somewhere?

The hi-fi shop on Wessington Boulevard was less than ten minutes' walk from their home. When Carol had not returned after half an hour, Mr Naisbitt felt anxious. The neighbourhood was not a rough one and Carol had the safety of the car, but it was still odd that she had not returned home, or even called, by now. Mr Naisbitt had been aware that Stan was helping out at the hi-fi store, so he had suggested that Carol called there first to see if Courtney was with his friend there.

Mr Naisbitt did not delay any longer after half an hour had passed but walked quickly to the hi-fi store. He saw his wife's car parked outside – an ominous sign. Why had she not returned home immediately with Courtney? Striving to control his trepidation, he entered the shop. His worst fears were confirmed when he saw that the drawer from the cash till had been wrenched open and was hanging out empty. A few coins lay on the floor. Where were his wife and his son? He called out, but there was no reply. Quickly he looked around; he had never been to the place before and did not know the layout. There was a door in back. He opened it and found that it led down a flight of stairs to the basement. He walked downstairs gingerly, for he had nothing with him he could use to ward off any possible assailant. A door to the left opened into a small kitchen, another door to a toilet. The third door was slightly ajar. He opened it, and before him lay the horror of the massacre. He rushed up the stairs to find the telephone, which mercifully had not been torn from its moorings, and dialled the police emergency number.

Ambulances rushed the five victims to hospital. Carol Naisbitt, Michelle Ansley and Stan Walker were found to be dead on arrival; the other two would survive. Orren Walker eventually made a good recovery, but Courtney's return to normality was long delayed. He had to undergo a series of major operations, and was left with both physical and psychological damage, but after two years he was able to return to his studies. The father of the family was devastated by the death of his wife and the long-drawn-out trauma to his son. He was comforted by Orren Walker whose son had shared in their common ordeal and died. The two men became good friends. Walker, who was an outgoing type, often felt like talking about the experiences they had gone through in the hi-fi store basement, but Naisbitt, a more introspective man, found the memories of his discovery there and the subsequent events too painful to discuss. He would steer Walker's conversation to other topics.

The topic, however, was on the lips of everyone in Ogden. Nothing like this had ever happened before in their little town, and the citizens were deeply shocked. The police were, of course, making an all-out effort to find the three responsible for the outrage, but the descriptions of the intruders given to them by the surviving victims were vague, not because they had not seen them clearly but because their communication was impaired by their horrific head injuries. The police knew little more than that there had been three robbers – two men and a youth. It seemed that the oldest-looking of the men, in his mid-twenties, had been the ringleader, and that the second man had merely done various things when told to do them by the first man. The youth was, apparently, little more than a boy, and had done nothing but just be there, as Courtney later put it. All three were black. None of them wore a mask or tried to disguise his voice. The surviving victims could not remember the clothes they wore, or their height or build.

From these sketchy descriptions, police were able to build up the profile of a suspect which matched that of a suspect who had been interrogated in connection with the murder in October of the previous year of a black airman at the nearby Hill Field USAF base. This man, Dale Pierre, aged twenty-five, had been released after the interrogation owing to lack of conclusive evidence, but his demeanour at the interrogation bore remarkable similarities to his reported behaviour in the basement as described by the two surviving victims. An anonymous informant, who was also an airman at the Hill Field base, tipped off the police that he had overheard two airmen, Dale Pierre and another named William Andrews, outlining a robbery they were planning to commit at a hi-fi shop in town. During the course of the conversation, the witness stated, Dale Pierre had remarked, 'One of these days when I rob a hi-fi shop I'm not gonna leave any witnesses. If anyone gets in my way I'm gonna kill 'em.'

Children playing on a garbage dump on ground opposite the air base and looking for returnable bottles found a wallet and a purse which had belonged to two of the hi-fi store victims. The barrack building nearest the dump was No. 351, which accommodated Dale Pierre, William Andrews and a third airman, Keith Roberts, who although he looked not a day over fifteen, was in fact nineteen. The police obtained a search warrant and went over their quarters with a fine toothcomb. Among other things, they found a rental agreement which Dale Pierre had signed on the day before the murders for a garage-store situated only a few blocks from the Wessington Boulevard store. Detectives broke into the locked store and found it stacked high with 24,000 dollars' worth of stolen hi-fi and stereo equipment. Incongruously, standing among the gleaming electronic units, was a half-empty bottle of Drano ....

The police wasted no further time. They arrested Dale

Pierre, twenty-one-year-old William Andrews and the baby-faced Keith Roberts and charged them all with first-degree murder. They were sent for trial at Farmington, Utah, since it would have been less than prudent to hold the trial in Ogden, whose citizens were, understandably enough, in an ugly mood.

The trial lasted a month. Dale Pierre and William Andrews were found guilty on all counts and sentenced to death; Roberts was acquitted of the murder charges but convicted of aggravated robbery. An execution date was set on five different occasions, but sentence was not carried out while appeal procedures were pending. Pierre and Andrews remain under maximum security in Utah State Prison, where Roberts is serving his term for robbery.

During the trial, a witness – a cinema attendant – described having admitted Pierre to a Clint Eastwood movie, *Magnum Force*, shortly before the hi-fi shop robbery. In this film, a pimp forces a prostitute to drink caustic drain-cleaning fluid, and she dies almost immediately. The movies, however, do not always reflect real-life situations accurately, and it is unlikely that a person who drank such a substance would die with such consummate speed. It is probably a safe conjecture that Dale Pierre decided to kill his five victims silently using this method, but that when he found to his dismay that the method would not work, he was forced to shoot them in order to silence them. It would seem that this is yet another example of the oft-repeated claim by killers that they were 'influenced by the movies'.

15

'Murder Decreases Natural Disasters'

On 18 April 1947, in Salinas, California, a boy was born who showed every promise of fulfilling the hopes of his devout Catholic parents. As a child he was well behaved, and at college he was an assiduous student and in fact the class of 1954 voted him the boy 'most likely to succeed'. When he was seventeen he got engaged to a girl, whom he treated with the utmost respect, earning in turn the respect of her parents, who considered him to be a good prospective match. Both sets of parents encouraged him to complete his studies and set his sights on university. The boy's name was Herbert Mullin.

Herb, as he was called, had a close male friend named Dean; they were devoted buddies and went everywhere together, attending all the college activities which interested them, and joining the college athletic clubs, including a group which called themselves the Zeros. They played football and baseball, jogged and swam. Herb's girlfriend sometimes complained that he spent more time with Dean than he did with her, but he would placate her with plausible excuses such as the activities they were attending were only for the college fraternity brothers.

In July 1965 Dean was killed in a motor accident, and Herb was inconsolable. He withdrew from all the college's extra-curricular activities, resigned his sports club and other society memberships, and shocked his girlfriend by telling her that he thought he might be homosexual. She wondered whether this was the reason why he had never put any pressure on her to have sexual intercourse with him, although he had previously told her that he was a virgin and wanted to wait until they were married for moral and religious reasons. He placed a photograph of Dean in a prominent position in his room and surrounded it with altar-like trappings such as a lace cloth and candles, making his room into a shrine to his dead friend.

The following year he became eligible for his call-up, and decided to become a conscientious objector. When his girlfriend heard about this she was very shocked and told her father, who was a military man, and doubtless under some pressure from him, she broke off her engagement.

His family had noted that Herb was becoming more and more withdrawn into himself and remote from reality, and they considered that his erratic behaviour had started after the death of Dean, which had dealt him a shattering blow. In February 1969 – he was then twenty-one – he told his family that he was going to India to study Eastern religions, but he did not go. He would talk about a project for several weeks, and then suddenly decide to abandon it.

One evening in March of the same year, during the course of a family dinner, he suddenly started to repeat every word his brother-in-law uttered, and to copy all his movements at table and afterwards. His family were extremely concerned at this show of neurotic behaviour, which Herb seemed unable to stop, and persuaded him to enter a mental hospital for a check-up on a voluntary basis. After six weeks of tests and treatment he was discharged as being 'an unco-operative patient' and, returning home, he continued to talk about yoga and to voice his religious feelings, although he no longer mentioned taking a trip to India. He had, however, stopped echoing his brother-in-law's speech and actions, and he did take the tablets the doctors had prescribed.

By October that year Herb had long since stopped taking his medication, and his behaviour had become more and more bizarre. He started to smoke pot and to take LSD and to hear voices inside his head which commanded him to do strange things, including shaving his head and burning his penis with a lighted cigarette. He was admitted to another mental hospital, where he was diagnosed as being a paranoid schizophrenic. While in hospital he wrote dozens of letters to people he had never met, signing himself 'Herb Mullin, the Human Sacrifice'. He was given various anti-psychotic drugs, and after a month he was discharged into the care of his parents, who were warned that he was not cured but that his disease of the mind could be kept under control provided that he took his tablets regularly.

Herb was not a little boy, and it was difficult for his parents to supervise the tablet-taking of an adult, especially one with such devious ways as their son. It is more than likely that Herb stopped taking them quite soon after his discharge, and it is known that he never went back for replacement supplies.

Much against his parents' advice, Herb decided to take a trip to Hawaii in June 1970. The purpose of the trip was never made clear but whatever this may have been in Herb's confused mind, he got into trouble of one kind and another and was committed to a mental hospital on the island. His parents were contacted and asked to send the money to pay for his fare home, which they did, and Herb was escorted on to the plane by a police officer.

Meanwhile, his parents had moved to another town in California, Santa Cruz. Home again with them, Herb started behaving strangely once again, and was soon in trouble with the police. When in June 1971 he told his parents that he was leaving home to go and live in San Francisco, they could not stop him, but they were extremely afraid that he might get into even more serious difficulties than he was in already. On the other hand, they were relieved that they did not have to contend with his bizarre daily exploits such as pouring water on the inside doormat, overturning his chair at table and sitting on the floor to eat his meals, and deliberately walking through puddles and mud.

His sojourn in San Francisco did not last long. He soon became fed up with living in cheap hotels, and he could not get a job because he was unemployable. He did in fact try a job as a dishwasher in a fast-food bar, but was dismissed after four hours when his employer found him stacking coke from the boiler on the plates. He then found a job pumping petrol in a garage, but walked out after one hour and forty minutes, giving no reason. He bummed around for a while, and then, in September 1972, after being evicted from his hotel for not paying his bill, he decided to hitch-hike home. His parents welcomed him with understandably mixed feelings ....

Their diffidence was justified. Shortly after his return home he showed every sign of being very disturbed, and said that he had received what he termed 'telepathic messages' ordering him to kill.

On 13 October 1972 he went out for a drive in his battered old car into a deserted stretch of highway which passed through the Santa Cruz Mountains. Along the way he saw an elderly tramp walking along at the side of the road. He stopped his car, and asked the man to have a look at his engine which he said was not performing as it should be, to see if he could see what was wrong. The unfortunate hobo fell for this ruse, lifted the hood and looked at the engine. As he was bending over the car, Herb came up behind him and hit him on the back of the head with a baseball bat, killing him instantly. He left the body where it lay – it was identified later as Lawrence White, aged seventy – and drove off home. When he arrived back, he put the car away, and, according to the later testimony of his parents, behaved as usual – 'normally' being not perhaps the right word, but he never gave any indication that he had killed a man.

On 24 October he was out again for another drive, and picked up a hitch-hiker, Mary Guilfoyle, who was a student at Cabrillo College. Driving towards Santa Cruz, he suddenly drew a hunting-knife and stabbed her through the heart. She slumped in the passenger seat dead. He drove on to a secluded part of the mountain road and lifted her body out of the car. He laid her at the side of the road and cut her body open from the base of the breastbone to the groin, and pulled out all her internal organs. Leaving her mutilated body to the vultures, he washed himself and the knife in a nearby stream, and drove home as if nothing had happened. It was four months before her skeleton was found and identified from dental records, and also from her clothes which had been scattered nearby.

A week after this latest murder, on 2 November, Herb entered the confessional box in St Mary's Church in Los Gatos. But it was not with the intention of confessing his ghastly deeds. The hunting knife which was his constant companion ('more trustworthy than any girl', he was later to say) was hidden beneath his coat. As Father Henri Tomei entered the confessional, Herb Mullin stabbed him to death with one blow. The Los Gatos community was outraged and police worked round the clock to try to apprehend Father Tomei's killer. However, the assassin had not been seen either entering or leaving the church, nor had anyone noticed his car outside.

By this time, Herb was now hearing voices in his head of potential victims begging him to kill them. In December 1972 he purchased a handgun, and on 25 January 1973 he heard a voice in his head commanding him to kill Jim Gianera, the man who many years previously had introduced him to marijuana. In Herb's disordered mind, Jim was asking Herb to kill him in retribution for having 'destroyed his (Herb's) mind'. He drove out to Branciforte Drive, where Jim had lived at the time, but he had moved. Kathy Francis, a twenty-nine-year-old divorcee who now lived at the address with her two small sons, told him Jim's new address in Santa Cruz. Herb lost no time in driving to the house where Jim Gianera now lived with his wife Carol Ann.

When Jim opened the door in response to Herb's knock, Herb shot him through the head. Carol Ann rushed from a rear room and dropped to her knees beside her husband's body. As she was bending over the corpse, Herb stabbed her in the back, then shot her. Leaving the front door wide open, he then jumped into his car and returned to the old address now occupied by Kathy Francis and her two little boys. The unsuspecting young woman opened the door in answer to Herb's knock, and asked him what he wanted. Without a word Mullin pushed past her into the house, turned and shot her in the back, then went upstairs and looked into the bedrooms. Kathy's two small children were in one of the rooms, sharing a double bed. Mullin shot them both dead.

During one of his rare moments of lucidity, Herb Mullin decided, on 30 January 1973 – only five days after murdering a man, two women and two children, four of whom he had never seen before in his life – to go and see a Lutheran minister in Santa Cruz. Mullin told the minister that he had problems – a mild word indeed to describe what was probably the understatement of the year – and said that 'Satan gets into people and makes them do things they don't want to do'. He did not elaborate, and it is not on record what the minister advised this man with a tortured mind to do. Whatever his advice had been, it seemed to have no beneficial effect, for only six days later he shot four teenage boys dead.

He had been walking aimlessly in the state park in Santa Cruz when he spotted a makeshift tent of plastic sheets and tarpaulins. Inside were four teenage boys sitting round a primus stove cooking a lunch of hamburgers and eggs and buttering rolls. The aroma of coffee wafted out.

'Hi!' one of them called out. 'Do you want some coffee?'

Herb ignored the invitation. 'You're camping illegally,' he said shortly. 'No camping's allowed in the state park.'

'Who are you?' another boy asked. 'You're not a park ranger – you're not wearing a badge.'

'I don't need a badge,' Herb replied. 'This will do.' And with these words he pulled out his gun. 'I'm going to have to report you all.'

The boys invited him inside and tried to talk him out of it, pointing out that they were doing no harm and not damaging the environment. They said that they were going home the following morning anyway. However, it was to no avail. The voices of death were once more pounding in Herb's brain. The boys must die, they said ... And, one after another, Herb shot them all.

His victim tally now stood at twelve. But there would be a thirteenth before he was apprehended and the senseless carnage halted.

Herb Mullin claimed his thirteenth victim on the thirteenth day of February. He was driving along towards his parents' home when he saw one of the elderly residents of the area tending his front garden. He stopped his car, walked up to the old man, drew his gun and shot him dead. The voices had urged him to kill this particular person, he later explained.

A woman in the house next door, hearing the shot, dashed to a window and, seeing her neighbour, Fred Perez, lying face down on his lawn and an old car moving off just outside, had the presence of mind to make a mental note of the description of the car and part of its number, and called police. Within minutes Herb Mullin had been arrested. He offered no resistance.

At his trial, Mullin endeavoured to explain the reasons for his killings. 'I saved thousands of lives from the San Francisco earthquake last year,' he said. When it was pointed out to him that there had been no earthquake in San Francisco in 1972, he said, 'Murder decreases natural disasters. By killing those people, I managed to avert the earthquake, so it never happened. I sacrificed the few to save the many.'

Despite this, Herb Mullin was judged to be legally sane, though it is indeed difficult to understand how, when his behaviour at the scenes of many of his murders is taken into account. For example, when he went into the church and shot Father Tomei, he left his car outside; it was broad daylight, and anyone could have seen it and noted its description and number. At the Gianera residence he left the front door wide open. At Kathy Francis's house, not content, as it were, with killing her, he went upstairs and shot dead two innocent children, aged four and seven, who could not possibly have done anybody any harm, much less this man whom they had never seen before. The four boys in the tent had been massacred in broad daylight, as too was Fred Perez, whom Mullin had casually approached, leaving his car at the side of the road. What sane man would commit murder in such a fashion? A sane murderer would at least try to hide his car and avoid daylight confrontations in populous residential neighbourhoods, and close doors after killing all the occupants of a house.

One is drawn inevitably to the conclusion that the jurists at Mullin's trial were under public pressure to show that justice was being done by finding guilty this man, who was as much a victim himself, and punishing him by life imprisonment. He was charged with a specimen ten murders. Although he will technically become eligible for parole in the year 2020, by which time he will be seventy-three, public opinion, being what it is and remembering the thirteen outrages, will almost certainly be brought to bear to persuade the authorities not to release him. So, instead of having received a course of psychiatric treatment, drugs, or even shock therapy or lobotomy, and then, his homicidal urges having been destroyed or at least safely controlled, being allowed to live out his last years and die in peace, he will languish and die in prison.

With the background of Herb Mullin's bizarre behaviour even before he started to commit murder, and given that he had already been incarcerated in three different mental hospitals and in at least one of them diagnosed as a paranoid schizophrenic, there had been enough early warning to have avoided the thirteen tragedies by keeping him in a secure mental hospital and giving him proper treatment until it was safe to discharge him, even if that were several years after his admission.

It is all too easy for the jurists to fly to their law books and ferret out the loopholes that enable them to categorize as sane a man who pours jugs of water on the inside doormat of his home, overturns chairs and eats on the floor, and leaves his car outside a church while he shoots a priest dead. The mind boggles ....

16

The Lampshade-maker

The hunting season was in full swing in Plainfield, a small farming community in Wisconsin. The deer season had just opened, and almost every farmer in the area was a dedicated hunter; many of them could rightfully be described as a crack shot. As well as the sport, the successful hunters would be able to enjoy bringing home venison for the table.

This time, the start of the 1957 hunting season would be marked by a hunting contest. A cash prize had been raised, which was to be awarded to the man who could bring down the heaviest buck with the biggest pair of antlers. The judge would be Bernard Muschinsky, the owner of the garage-cum-service depot. He had borrowed a large weighing-machine, which he set up just outside the door of his office.

On Friday night, 15 November 1957, the eve of the day of the hunting contest, at about 8 o'clock Ed Gein, one of the farmers, drove into the little town in his Ford pick-up. As he passed the garage he waved a friendly greeting to Muschinsky, who was ruling up a log-book in which to enter the names of the hunters, the weights and antler sizes of their trophies. Although Ed Gein called himself a farmer and lived on a farm, he did little, if any, farming. He had inherited the 275-acre farm on the death of his father in 1940, ever since which time he had gradually been selling off parcels of the land, until by 1957 only 160 acres remained, and even then he was in negotiation with a neighbour about a further sale. He spent most of his time drinking beer, reading pulp magazines, and driving around in his old car. But he was never averse to helping his neighbours with their projects such as building or repairing farm outbuildings, or tinkering with their cars or tractors when they proved troublesome.

Ed parked his car in front of Bernice Worden's general store. Bernice was serving behind the counter; her son Frank, who was deputy sheriff, was cleaning and oiling his shot-gun ready for the big hunt on the morrow.

'Hi!' Bernice said. 'What can I do for you?'

'I need some anti-freeze,' Ed replied. 'And now that I'm here, I'll have some ice-cream and some beer. I'll take those now, but the anti-freeze I can pick up in the morning. What time will you be open? Or are you going hunting with Frank?'

This latter remark was not made in jest. Bernice was an experienced hunter and a good shot.

'No, I'm not going,' the woman replied. 'Frank's the only one who is going. So there must be somebody to mind the store.'

Frank looked up from his shot-gun. 'I'm going to bag the biggest buck ever shot in this county,' he said with a grin, 'and I'll buy you all a beer with the prize money!'

'I wish you luck, Frank!' Ed said genially. 'I'll be in about eight o'clock for the anti-freeze. 'Bye for now.' He shuffled out, chuckling to himself at the young deputy sheriff's optimism. Then he headed for his favourite tavern.

The day of the hunt dawned, grey with a decidedly frosty bite in the air. The streets of Plainfield were deserted. The men and their shot-guns had long departed for the woods, on foot, on horseback, or by car. Bernard Muschinsky, sitting in his office with the weighing-machine and the log-book at the ready to await the returning marksmen, glanced idly up and looked out of the window. He saw Bernice Worden cross the street from the direction of her home and unlock the front door of her lock-up shop. Bernard looked at the clock. It was just coming up to eight o'clock. He returned to the paperwork on his desk and forgot about Bernice Worden.

The next time Bernard Muschinsky looked up it was 9.30, when he had to go outside to pump petrol into a customer's car. While he was doing so, happening to glance at the store opposite, he saw one of his farmer neighbours go up to the door, rattle the knob and, finding that the shop was closed, go away again. Muschinsky remembered that he had seen Bernice Worden open the store an hour and a half earlier, and wondered idly why she had shut up shop. Perhaps she had nipped out to purchase some item she needed, or even gone home, not feeling well. Still, it was really no concern of his. He shrugged and turned his attention to the petrol pump.

A little later, he was wondering, as he sat in his office, who among the hunters would be the first to bring in his buck to be weighed and measured, when a sudden sound caused him to look up. It was the Wordens' delivery truck driving off from the rear of the store. So Bernice had been there after all, he thought. Probably packing some deliveries and now she was taking them to a customer herself, because her son was not around. Yes, that was it. How stupid of him not to have thought of that in the first place!

At eleven o'clock, the first of the hunters arrived at Bernard Muschinsky's place for the weigh-in and antler measurement with his buck. It certainly was some buck – fat and in prime condition. The hunter, Elmo Weeks, considered that he had as good a chance as anyone else of winning the contest.

'Where did you catch him?' asked Muschinsky.

'Right on the edge of Ed Gein's land,' replied Weeks. 'Came right out into the open. A sitting target.'

'It's a mighty fine buck,' Muschinsky conceded, 'but you know Ed Gein takes a very dim view of anyone hunting on his property.'

'Ah, yes, I'll have to square things with him,' Weeks said. 'I'll take him a haunch of venison. It's a very funny thing, though, Bernie. I saw Ed while I was out there, just after I'd shot it, I dunno what time it was exactly. He was charging along the road at a terrific speed – at least fifty miles an hour. Never seen him drive that fast afore – usually even a gopher could outrun his car the way he drives. As he went past he saw me. Didn't look a bit put out to see me on his land. Stuck his hand out of the window of the car and waved to me.'

'That's certainly out of character for Ed,' Muschinsky said. 'Still, there's no telling with him. Bit of an oddball, that one, if you ask me.'

After Weeks had returned home, carved a haunch of venison and taken it to Ed's place, he returned to Muschinsky's service depot to fill up with petrol. 'Guess what, Bernie,' he said. 'When I got to Ed's place, there he was changing the tyres on his car. He'd taken off the snow-treads and was replacing them with regular tyres. Now, if that wasn't the goddam craziest thing you ever saw! He must be a nutcase to do that at this time of the year! What do you make of it, Bernie?'

'I can't imagine,' Muschinsky replied. 'It's just one of those crazy things Ed likes to do. How did he take it about your hunting on his land?'

'Oh, he didn't seem to mind at all,' the other man said. 'He was mighty pleased with the venison. Seemed to be in a good mood. He didn't ask me in, though – he never does. So I went off home.'

Shortly after dusk that evening, Ed Gein had another caller. The visitor was Bob Hill, another neighbour. He knocked at the farmhouse door, but there was no answer. He tried the doorknob, but it was locked. He walked round to the back of the house. In an outbuilding behind the house he could see the flickering of a lantern. As Bob approached, the light went out suddenly and Ed Gein appeared, closing the door of the outbuilding behind him.

'Hi, Ed,' Bob called. 'My car has broken down and I wonder if you could drive me into town? Dad's not back from hunting yet.'

'Sure,' Gein replied. 'Get into my car out front. I'll be right there.' Bob turned and made his way to where the old car stood. As he did so he heard the sound of a key being turned in the lock, followed by a heavy bolt being slid into place. Moments later, Ed Gein slid behind the wheel and drove young Bob into town, then returned home.

At six o'clock Bernard Muschinsky was sitting in his office studying the figures in the log-book. He had weighed and measured a couple of dozen deer and all the entries had not yet come in. A shadow fell across his desk from the open doorway, and he looked up to see Frank Worden.

'Hi!' he said. 'Where's your buck?'

Frank leaned his shot-gun against the wall with a look of disgust. 'I never even saw a deer the whole day,' he said. 'I never had a chance to fire a single shot. Big deal!'

'Never mind, Frank,' Muschinsky said. 'It's not the end of the world.'

Frank Worden was looking intently at his mother's store across the road. 'There are no lights on in the shop!' he exclaimed. 'Did Mom close early? Unusual for her to do that – she usually stays open till eight o'clock at least.'

Muschinsky followed the young man's gaze. 'That's funny,' he said. 'I know she opened up at eight o'clock this morning – I saw her with my own eyes. Then later on some guy tried to get in but found the door locked, and went away again. Later on I saw your delivery truck drive out from the back. I haven't seen your mother since I saw her opening up this morning.'

'Maybe she went home because she wasn't feeling too good,' the young man replied. He fished in his pockets for his keys. 'I don't seem to have the store keys with me,' he said. 'I'll go home and see if Mom's there.' Picking up his shot-gun, he went down the few wooden steps from Bernard's office, got into his car and drove off with a wave.

Fifteen minutes later he was back again. 'Mom's not at home,' he reported. 'It doesn't even look as though she'd been home at all. I've got my store keys now – I'm going over to take a look. Will you come with me in case anything's wrong?'

'Sure.' Muschinsky took his jacket off its peg and locked the office, and the two men crossed the street to Worden's General Stores. Frank Worden unlocked the door and entered, followed closely by Bernard Muschinsky. Then Worden gasped in horror. 'My God, that's blood!' He pointed to the dark trail leading from the counter, across the floor and towards the rear door. The cash register was missing.

'We'd better get Art down here quick,' Bernard said. 'It looks like there's been a burglary and something's happened to your mother.'

Art was Arthur Schley, the sheriff of Wautoma County, based at Wautoma, fifteen miles away. He immediately set out for Plainfield. When he entered the store he found Bernard Muschinsky trying to comfort a distraught Frank Worden.

The sheriff was frankly puzzled. If this was a robbery, why had the thief taken the heavy cash register with him? Normally break-in thieves just prised open the till and made off with the money. And if there had been a murder, why would he have taken the body with him? These two points were something quite new in his experience. Not that there was much crime in Wautoma County, a rural area of hard-working farmers of Dutch and German extraction.

Muschinsky told the sheriff how he had seen Bernice Worden opening the store that morning, and of the delivery truck being driven off. 'If the person driving the truck had been the burglar,' Schley remarked, 'it would surely have been difficult to drive off with the cash register and possibly a dead body, without being spotted by someone.'

Worden had regained some of his composure by this time, but he winced at the mention of a dead body. 'There weren't many folks in town this morning,' he pointed out. 'All the men were out hunting, and most of the women stay at home in the morning cooking. When they go to the shops, they usually don't go until after lunch and the kids have gone back to school. Let's have a look at the sales book. Mom always records all sales and the names of the customers.' He went behind the counter and took the book from a drawer.

Turning to that day's date – 16 November 1957 – and looking up, he said, 'Mom seems to have had only one customer today – Ed Gein, anti-freeze, paid 99 cents.' In a moment, he had remembered. 'Last night,' he continued, 'Ed came into the shop, bought some beer and ice-cream, and said he'd be in at eight o'clock this morning to pick up some anti-freeze.'

'OK, we'll drive out and talk to Ed and see if he knows anything,' Schley said, 'but first I'd like to look around the shop.' He walked over to a gun-rack which held a number of shot-guns and rifles of various calibres. 'See that?' he said, pointing to a rifle. 'It's been taken out and put back the wrong way round.' The magazine was facing inwards; all the rest were facing outwards. Schley took the gun from the rack and sniffed the barrel. 'It's been fired recently,' he said. He pulled back the bolt. A .22 shell clattered to the floor. 'This looks like the weapon which ...' He stopped in mid-sentence as he caught Frank Worden's anguished look. 'Perhaps your mother's only been wounded,' he said. 'But where is she?' He took the rifle with him. 'The fingerprint boys will have to give this a going over,' he said. He picked up the ejected shell and put it into a bag before putting it in his pocket.

Schley led the way to where the blood trail led to the rear door, which had been left unlocked. The trail led to the spot where the Wordens' delivery truck was usually parked. There he stopped abruptly. The van was nowhere in sight.

'OK, Frank, you're the deputy sheriff here, so you'd better come with me. We'll just go over to Ed Gein's farm to see if he knows anything. He may very well be the last person to have seen your mother before – before she disappeared.'

Thanking Muschinsky for his help, the two men moved off in the sheriff's car. When they reached the Gein farm, no lights were visible.

'He's probably out,' Frank said. 'Usually goes out drinking beer on a Saturday night. Drinks at home on ordinary week-days usually. Keeps to himself a lot, he does.'

'Doesn't work the farm either, it seems,' observed Schley, sweeping a hand round the silent fields, devoid of livestock or arable crops. 'How does he earn a living?'

'He sells off the land a bit at a time and lives on the proceeds,' Frank replied.

'Waste of good land,' said the sheriff. 'He's not all that old, is he?'

'Fifty or so, I should think,' Frank replied. Ed Gein was in fact fifty-one years of age.

After pounding on the front door of the farmhouse, it soon became obvious that Ed was not at home. 'We'll take a look round,' the sheriff proposed.

The two men walked round to the rear of the house, finding the back door also locked. Then they turned their attention to the outbuilding facing the back of the house – the one from which Bob Hill had seen Gein emerge some time earlier.

The main door was locked and bolted, but at the rear was another door, which was unlocked. Gein had obviously forgotten to lock it in his haste. Schley pushed it wide open, entered and took a flashlight from his pocket. What he saw within its beam made his stomach churn. 'Don't come in here, Frank!' he called out in what sounded like a strangled voice. 'Stay outside!'

But it was too late. Frank had entered, close behind the sheriff. His mother's body was hanging upside-down from a beam in the ceiling from two meat-hooks through her feet. She was stark naked and her body had been eviscerated. She had also been decapitated, but Frank recognized her from a large mole on her forearm and a 'fingerstall' bandage on her right ring finger which she had cut the previous day when opening a can. Her clothes, too, lay strewn about the floor.

Frank Worden uttered the wild cry of a man in anguish. Then he rushed from the building out into the night and flung himself face down on the grass. Choking sobs racked his body.

Arthur Schley, looking round inside the building with his torch beam seeking out the dark corners, soon found what he was looking for. Bernice Worden's head, neatly packaged in plastic, stared at him from a shelf. The top of the head had been sawn off just above the browline, and the skull had been hollowed out and stuffed with newspaper. Schley walked from the carnage as rapidly as he could and slammed the door behind him.

At the sound, Frank Worden jumped to his feet. 'Art,' he cried urgently, 'I'm going home for my shot-gun, and then I'm going to find Ed. Then you can arrest *me* for murder, too.'

Schley took Frank by the shoulders. 'Frank, I know just how you feel, believe me. But that will not do any good. Two wrongs don't make a right. Ed will be brought to trial. We don't have Old Sparky any more in Wisconsin – but he'll get life. And I mean life. They'll never let him out.'

Worden shook off the restraining grasp. 'Let me go!' he cried. 'This is my thing I have to do. I'm going for my gun.'

'I'm sorry, Frank', the sheriff replied quietly, 'but I can't let you do this. Get into my car. I'm going to drop you off home, and you must stay there. Then I'm going to get Ed Gein.' Schley steered Frank Worden into his car, where the young man collapsed sobbing in a crumpled heap.

After leaving Frank at his home, Schley went to look for Gein. He found him eventually at the home of one of his friends, where he was enjoying a substantial meal of German sausage, sauerkraut, pickled gherkins and onions, followed by cheese and cookies and a mug of steaming coffee. He had just about finished his meal when Arthur Schley entered the room with gun drawn.

'All right, Ed,' he said. 'Get your coat. You're coming with me.'

'Hey, Art – what's all this?' Gein said, looking up. 'Where and what for?'

'The county jail in Wautoma.'

'The county jail in Wautoma? Why, what have I done now?'

'We'll talk about it there. Get your coat. If you stay here, you'll be lynched – that's for sure. I've just come from the workshop at the back of your house, Ed.'

Gein rose from the table and reached for his jacket. He was as calm as he looked. Schley was the one whose hands shook as he handcuffed the older man.

'OK, OK,' Gein said. 'You're the law. If you say I have to go to Wautoma, then I guess I have to go to Wautoma.' He turned to his friend who was still drinking his coffee. 'Sorry about all this, old buddy. Probably some misunderstanding. See you soon.' He shrugged in a gesture of well-feigned bewilderment.

Before leaving, the sheriff telephoned headquarters. He ordered two of his deputies and the fingerprint men to go at once to the Gein farmhouse. 'Don't be too surprised at what you'll find there,' he said. 'I'll join you later.'

Early on Sunday morning, Schley and his men were joined by a mobile unit from the state crime laboratory at Madison, the state capital, including Charles Wilson, the laboratory chief and two of his top investigators, Jan Beck and James Halligan. The sheriff of adjoining Portage County also joined them. He was interested in the three-year-old disappearance of Mary Hogan, a fifty-four-year-old widow who, although a native of Portage County, had opened a tavern at Bancroft, some six miles from the Gein farm. Ed had patronized her tavern frequently up to the day she disappeared – 9 December 1954. All that was known was that Mary Hogan had closed the tavern at midnight on 9 December, when only two customers remained. One had left; the other was Ed Gein. Sheriff Herbert had never closed the case … Mary Hogan seemed to have vanished into thin air. Her bed had not been slept in; none of her property or clothing was missing, and the money in the till had not been touched.

Some weeks later, Ed Gein had been working, on and off, for Elmo Weeks, the hunter who had shot his deer on the edge of Ed's land. Elmo owned the local sawmill and had known Gein for twenty years. The two men talked as they worked.

'If you'd persuaded Mary to marry you,' Elmo said, 'she'd be alive and cooking – cooking for you, that is!'

'You sound like you're sure she's dead,' Gein replied.

'Must be. Mary wasn't the type to just go off somewhere and leave everything, with just the clothes she stood up in. Didn't even take her handbag. Now where can you find a woman who goes off anywhere at all without taking her handbag?'

'Maybe she *is* a handbag,' said Gein enigmatically.

'What the hell are you talking about?' Elmo said. 'You and your jokes! Like I said – if you'd paid more attention to courting her, instead of thinking up your jokes, you'd have a nice little wife now. And by Jeez, she was a good cook, I can tell you. She used to cook meals for customers like nobody's business. They'd come from miles around. Anybody'd think they were starving, the way they'd come for the meals as well as the beer.' Elmo patted his ample stomach. 'I wonder who it was knocked her off? Did a real disservice to the community.'

'She's down at my house right now,' Gein said.

'Aw, quit horsing around!' Elmo said. 'Come on! We've got work to do!'

Later, Elmo was to remember Gein's apparent jesting, when it was found that Gein had not been 'horsing around' after all ....

Meanwhile, at the Gein farm, the various law enforcement officers were confronted with what must surely be the most ghastly array of exhibits in the history of crime. The outbuilding appeared to have been used as a workshop of horror, and the products transferred to various rooms in the rambling old house. Various parts of an estimated dozen female bodies were found. Ten human skulls lay around on various shelves. A cardboard box containing human noses was found in the kitchen, and on the stove was a pan of water containing a human heart.

Half a dozen women's faces had been skinned and made into realistic masks, all well-preserved, complete with hair. In the dining-room were four chairs upholstered with human skin. The officers also found a tom-tom drum made from a two-quart can, the top and bottom of which had been knocked out and replaced with tautly-stretched human skin.

In every room was a lampshade, in which human skin had taken the place of parchment. And on a table in one room was a handbag, made from human skin.

Hardened officers rushed from the house to vomit, and two deputies had to be sent home and others called out to replace them. The crime lab men carefully packed the hideous exhibits in labelled boxes and bags and loaded the grisly cargo into the mobile unit to be transported to Madison.

Sheriff Herbert recalled that, some years previous to her disappearance, Mary Hogan had been involved in a motoring accident, after which she had had several X-rays taken of her head for a suspected skull fracture. The X-rays revealed a fracture which had left a permanent internal bone scar. No doubt, Herbert surmised, Mary Hogan's doctor would still have these X-ray plates, and if he could obtain these he would be able to check them against skulls found on the Gein premises. His surmise proved correct, and one of the skulls matched the plates.

In custody, Gein confessed to the murder of Mary Hogan and also to killing the forty-eight-year-old widow Bernice Worden. When asked why he had taken the cash register, since he was not short of money, he replied, 'There was a sum of forty-one dollars in the till. But I never took the money. I took the register to play with. I just liked to enjoy watching the way it added up all the items on the paper roll inside.' The interrogators shook their heads slowly in disbelief. But more was yet to come ....

'There were parts of about twelve bodies found at your farmhouse,' the interrogators continued. 'That makes ten so far unaccounted for. When did you murder them? And who were they?'

'Oh, but I didn't kill them,' Gein said calmly in a matter-of-fact voice. 'I dug them up out of their graves in the cemetery.'

'You *what*?' The questioners thought that they were not hearing him correctly.

'I'd read the obituary notices in the papers, then I'd go to the cemetery in the middle of the night and dig up the body. No one saw me go, or come back. I had a compulsion to do it. It all started after my mother died in 1945. I felt I wanted to change my sex and become a woman. I used to skin the bodies and wear the skin. I'd make a mask from the face. Then I felt I was really like the woman I wanted to be. I liked to wear women's hair, too – I'd wear a scalp like a wig. I enjoyed cutting up the bodies and sorting out the inside parts, too. Once I made a vest [waistcoat] out of a woman's skin. I'd oil the skins and faces to prevent them from drying out. I'd wear them round the house. Do you think I could have a cup of coffee?' An officer at this point hurriedly left the interrogation room, but it was not to fetch coffee ....

After partaking of refreshment, Gein continued with his grisly saga of incredible savagery. He described how he had butchered and eviscerated the widow from the general store, collecting her blood in buckets and emptying them down the toilet. He considered smoking and shrinking her head, using the same methods as those used by the Jivaro Indians described in one of his books. The book in question was found in his house along with several manuals of anatomy, syringes, a gallon container of embalming fluid and other items which bore mute witness to his ghoulish pre-occupations.

'I still hadn't quite made up my mind about that,' he continued, 'when I decided to go over to [my friend's] place for supper. His wife cooks wonderful German food, you know.'

The flabbergasted law enforcement officers returned Gein to his cell, and sat down to try to recover their composure. Gein, it was decided, was to be taken to Madison to undergo a lie-detector test. The findings seemed to point to his having told the truth ....

On the morning of Friday, 22 November, Gein appeared before Judge Herbert A. Bunde in Wautoma, where he was remanded in custody pending psychiatric examination. The judge, on learning that Gein had no counsel, appointed him a local attorney, William Belter, who pleaded not guilty by reason of insanity on his client's behalf. Judge Bunde then directed that Gein be held at the Central State Hospital at Waupun for a period of thirty days to undergo psychiatric examination. And Sheriff Arthur Schley refused to allow any reporters to interview Gein in the secure ward of the hospital.

A complication now arose. Just as Elmo Weeks had laughed and refused to believe any of Gein's outrageous claims, the good folks of Plainfield, whose loved ones were interred in the local cemetery, refused to believe that their family members had been dug up and dissected and otherwise violated. They preferred to believe that the corpses put together from Gein's macabre collection were those of strangers, rather than concede that they were own kith and kin.

A very small minority, however, disagreed with this general view. They demanded that two of the graves Gein had mentioned in his confessions be opened, in order to ascertain whether Gein's claims were true or just empty boasts. The group was led by Ralph Wing, a member of the Plainfield town council. After a good deal of argument on both sides, the authorities eventually agreed, albeit reluc-tantly, to this proposal. However, they refused to allow the full list of names obtained from Gein to be published.

The two graves opened were those of Eleanor Adams, a

seventy-year-old widow who had died in 1951, and Mabel Everson, sixty-eight, who had also died the same year, on 15 April. When Mrs Adams's casket was pulled to the surface, it was found to be empty. Then Mrs Everson's casket was raised. It contained a rusted crowbar, and a few bones. Gein had been telling the truth. He had used an iron crowbar to prise open coffins, and on a few occasions he had revisited graves and returned a few of their bones to the coffins. This he had mentioned at one point in the lengthy narrative of his confessions, although he was apparently unable to account for any reason why he did this on a small number of occasions.

It was agreed that no more graves should be opened, but now the time had come to decide what was to be done with the Ghoul of Plainfield. Although some people thought confinement for life in a mental institution would be appropriate, a far greater number wanted him to stand trial and serve life in prison, since there was no death penalty in Wisconsin.

Under Wisconsin law, a judge could order the commitment of a prisoner to determine his sanity. After this thirty-day observation period, the judge could then act on the basis of the hospital report. It was up to the judge to decide whether the prisoner should remain in the hospital for treatment, or whether he was sane under the legal definition of the term and fit to stand trial.

At the end of the thirty-day period, Judge Bunde declared that the observations of the psychiatrists had led them to pronounce Gein insane and incompetent to stand trial. But Judge Bunde decided that further expert testimony was required, considering that thirty days was really an insufficient period of time to arrive at any permanent conclusion. Many people, understandably, were more than a little nonplussed at Judge Bunde's opinion. How many more corpses, they argued, would Gein have had to butcher, dissect and make lampshades out of before he was considered completely mad?

Psychiatrists treated and examined Ed Gein and reported to the judge, who still could not make a firm decision and referred the question of Gein's sanity back to the doctors, for the next ten years. Then, one day early in 1968, Dr E.F. Schubert, the Superintendent of the Central State Hospital, advised Judge Frank Gollmar – Judge Bunde by that time having retired – that their patient was now mentally competent to stand trial and even to assist in his own defence.

Because of the passage of time, the prosecution of Gein would present unavoidable problems. Sheriff Arthur Schley had died, as had other key witnesses. However, some of the original protagonists were still available, including Sheriff Herbert and Charles Wilson, the head of the crime lab. But the attorney who had represented Gein at the original hearing was no longer practising, and the Attorney-General of Wisconsin appointed Dominic Frinzi as his successor. The prosecutor would be Robert Sutton. Some of the items preserved as evidence which had been removed from the house of horror had had to be destroyed, but these had been photographed; other items were still available. Gein's methods of preservation had been very good ....

The date for the new trial was 7 November 1968. Prosecutor Sutton put on the stand several witnesses who had been in the Gein farmhouse at the time the horrific discoveries had been made. One crime lab technician testified that Gein had confessed to the murder of Bernice Worden in his presence. Sheriff Herbert testified that he had seen about ten heads and that one of these looked like the head of Mary Hogan, whom he knew. And Charles Wilson testified that a .32 calibre bullet found in Mary Hogan's tavern had been fired from a .32 calibre pistol found in the Gein house.

After hearing all the evidence, the prosecution considered that Gein was guilty of first-degree murder. But the defence contended that, even if Gein were now legally sane and fit to stand trial, he had been insane at the time he murdered Bernice Worden. Two psychiatrists, including Dr Schubert, reinforced this finding.

On 14 November Judge Gollmar ruled that Gein had indeed been insane at the time of the killing, and ordered him re-committed for life to the Central State Hospital. He knew that the doctors, knowing all the facts, would never dare release him.

The citizens of Plainfield were well aware of this, and peace of mind now descended on them, for themselves and for those of their families who lay buried in Plainfield

Cemetery. But first of all they had to exorcize the dreadful evil that had been in their midst, all unknown to them, for so long. They went as one body to the Gein farmhouse and burned it to the ground.

On Thursday, 26 July 1984, Ed Gein died in his solitary room in the secure ward of the Central State Hospital, of natural causes. He was seventy-seven. No cemetery or churchyard would accept his body, so he was cremated and his ashes scattered to the four winds. No mourners attended the ceremony which ended the earthly career of the man they used to call the Lampshade-maker.

17

A View from the Tower

Up to the age of twenty-five, Charles Whitman's behaviour had been perfectly normal. He had certainly come to hate his father, who was a harsh authoritarian, beating his wife and children when the mood took him, but Charles himself had not shown any overt mental disturbance, whatever he might have been feeling inside. He would try to keep out of his father's way if he sensed that one of his rages was impending and that he was likely to be at the receiving end of a leather strap for no reason.

As soon as he was old enough he left the family home in Florida and moved to Austin, Texas, where first he joined the Marines for a spell, becoming a crack marksman. After he left that service he married a girl named Kathleen Binney, and enrolled in the University of Texas to study architectural engineering.

In late 1965 his mother decided that enough was enough and left her husband. She moved to Austin, in order to be nearer to her son and daughter-in-law. Soon after the move, Charles began to be afflicted by severe headaches, verging on migraine, and showed signs of increasingly erratic behaviour. His friends at the university noticed that he had been acting strangely for some time, and one of his colleagues suggested that he go and see the campus psychiatrist, Dr Maurice Heatly, for counselling, which he did. He arranged an appointment for 29 March, and frankly told Dr Heatly about what he termed the 'manic rages' which swept over him from time to time, and which led him occasionally to assault his wife. Kathleen seemed very tolerant, he said, because she realized that Charles was suffering some kind of mental disturbance. Dr Heatly noted that Charles seemed 'full of aggression and hostility'. Another appointment was made for a fortnight later, but before the date which had been fixed Charles cancelled his appointment, stating that he had decided to 'fight it out alone' ....

On 31 July 1966 his lonely fight came to a head. He sat down in his apartment to write what was virtually a suicide note. 'I do not fully understand what is compelling me to type this note,' he began. 'I went to see a psychiatrist on 29 March. I have been having strange fears and violent impulses. I've had some tremendous headaches in the past. I am prepared to die. I am going to kill my wife first. After my death, I wish an autopsy to be performed on me to see if there's any mental disorder. I hate my father, and life is not worth living.'

After he had completed the typed suicide note, he spent several hours talking with friends, who later stated that his behaviour at the time was quite normal. He then went to pick up his wife from work and left her at their apartment. Later that evening, after driving his wife to a college evening class, he went to his mother's apartment, stabbed her in the chest and then shot her in the back of the head. Returning to his own home, he took the suicide note out of the drawer where he had hidden it, put it back into the typewriter and added: 'I have just killed my mother. If there's a heaven she's going there. If there's not a heaven, she's out of her pain and misery.' He then put the letter back into the drawer. Later he picked up his wife in the car and brought her home. She complained of feeling unwell and went to bed early, leaving Charles brooding in the kitchen over his coffee.

He added yet a further sentence to his suicide note: 'I loved my mother with all my heart.' Then he took a knife and walked into the bedroom and stabbed his wife to death as she slept.

The following morning Charles Whitman armed himself with several pistols and a powerful 33mm Remington rifle, stuffing his pockets with ammunition. He also took a supply of food and water. On his way to the tower on the university campus, he stopped out at a gunsmith's to purchase a .30 calibre carbine and several boxes of ammunition. Stuffing this veritable arsenal of weapons into a duffel bag which he still had from his days in the Marines, he continued purposefully to the tower, which is twenty-seven floors and 300 ft. high and has a commanding view over the entire campus of the University of Texas. He rented a small trolley to enable him to transport all his gear up to the twenty-seventh floor, to the observation deck at the top of the tower.

There he encountered the receptionist, Edna Townsley, who asked him what he wanted. His answer was to shatter her skull with one blow of the rifle butt. A young couple appeared, just as he had dragged Mrs Townsley's body behind a desk. The young girl grimaced in disgust at the sight of the pool of blood on the floor, and her companion said that someone must have had a very bad nosebleed, as they skirted round the blood. They did not say anything to Whitman, who smiled at them, and they smiled back. Whitman made no move to harm them, and they walked past him, unaware of their close brush with death ....

A nineteen-year-old youth, Mike Gabor, came into view, followed by his mother, Ella Gabor, and his aunt, Marguerite Lamport. Whitman killed the youth with a single blast from the shot-gun. He then shot the two women, killing the boy's aunt and wounding his mother. The husbands of the two women, walking close behind them, realized that they were confronting a maniac. Incredibly, Whitman made no attempt to shoot them or to prevent them from carrying the bodies down the stairs to summon aid.

At precisely 11.48 a.m. Charles Whitman barricaded himself on the tower walkway and began shooting at random anyone within range of his sights. Clare Wilson, who was pregnant, fell with a bullet in her abdomen. She survived, but her unborn baby was killed. Next, nineteen-year-old Thomas Eckman was killed instantly with a single shot as he knelt beside Clare Wilson to render first aid.

The tower was quickly surrounded by police, and a light plane was sent up with a police marksman to try to shoot the mad sniper who spelt death to any unsuspecting person walking on the campus 300 feet below. But the deadly accuracy of the ex-Marine was far too great a hazard and the plane was ordered to descend. Whitman continued shooting with impunity, and in little more than an hour from when he had started shooting from the tower, he had killed sixteen and wounded another thirty. More than a hundred policemen returned his fire, but not one was able to hit his target. It was then decided to try more desperate tactics.

A small group of three officers, led by patrolman Ramiro Martinez, made their way inconspicuously up to the floor of the tower below the one where the demented sniper was ensconced among his barrage of weapons. Absorbed in his frenzy, Whitman had not heard or noticed their stealthy approach. Suddenly and without warning, at a given signal from Ramiro Martinez, the group charged, killing Whitman in a hail of bullets. Martinez was wounded by a shot from Whitman, but recovered.

On that morning of 1 August 1966, the crazed sniper had killed a total of twenty-one persons and wounded thirty-one, taking into account the murder of his wife and mother, the killing of Mrs Townsley, Mike Gabor and Marguerite Lamport, and the wounding of Martinez.

Charles Whitman's wish for an autopsy was granted. When his bullet-riddled body was brought in for post-mortem, an examination of his brain revealed the presence of a tumour pressing on the amygdaloid nucleus, which is the brain's aggression centre.

Later, when Dr Heatly's notes were produced in evidence at the inquest, the following sentence was revealed, dated four months before the killings: 'At one point he [Whitman] said he had a frequent fantasy of taking a deer rifle up to the top of the tower and sniping at passers-by.' Who knows what the outcome would have been if only Whitman had kept that second appointment with Dr Heatly – and subsequent appointments? The possibility of a brain tumour might have suggested itself. An X-ray would certainly have revealed it – and prompt surgical intervention could have saved twenty-one lives – not to mention Charles Whitman's own. He had the intelligence to realize that there was something seriously wrong with his mind, and to go and seek help. But the reason, or reasons, why he subsequently decided to 'go it alone' and spurn further treatment, will never be known.

18

A Matter of Family Honour

The true crime buff who has made a study of the history of what are popularly dubbed 'trunk murders' will scarcely have failed to note two factors common to most of them: firstly, that they are closely associated with railway transport, and secondly, that in a good many of them the bodies were dismembered. With regard to this second feature, however, it has occurred to me that the vast majority of those murders in which the victims' bodies were dismembered took place in more recent historical times, while those of an earlier period were rarely so mutilated; and thinking more about this topic, the reason must surely be that in the good old days trunks – usually called portmanteaus – were huge and unwieldy contraptions that more often than not needed the strength of two or more men to lift them, whereas these days such monstrosities are a rarity and nowadays travellers prefer to use much smaller suitcases, which are both more convenient and easier on the arms.

John Robinson, who in 1927 murdered Mrs Minnie Bonati, had no difficulty at all in cramming the hefty eleven-stone Mrs Bonati whole into a trunk. The latter was so big that, even when empty, he had to request the assistance of the conductor in getting it on to the bus after he had purchased it from a shop in Brixton. Then, after Mrs Bonati had been transferred to it, he had to ask the cab-driver to help him hoist the trunk on to his cab. When the driver had commented on its weight, Robinson had told him that it was full of books.

Tony Mancini, too, in 1933, was able to stuff the complete body of his mistress, Violette Kaye, into a trunk which he left in his Brighton room. And Arthur Devereux, in 1905, was able to stow not only the body of his wife but also those of two of his children into a single trunk, which was large and heavy enough to have forced him to hire a delivery van to transport it to the warehouse where he deposited it.

But in the case, or rather cases, for there were two – which forms the subject of this chapter, the year was 1968 and huge cabin trunks were not normally used except, perhaps, by persons shipping goods overseas in the process of emigration, or on a long extended cruise. These were dealt with by shipping companies who of course employed their own transport to deal with them. An ordinary citizen travelling by bus or train would look very conspicuous indeed if he were to be seen humping a huge cabin trunk about. So a murderer wishing to dispose of a body, unable to get it into even a largish average-size suitcase, would have no choice but to dismember his victim's body and divide it between two suitcases – in this instance with a duffel bag thrown in for the head.

On 5 April 1968 two train drivers going off duty at Wolverhampton railway station noticed a suitcase which had been left in an empty compartment of a railway carriage in the train which had just arrived from London. Naturally they assumed some absent-minded passenger had forgotten it, and took it in to the lost property office. No one claimed it, and it was decided to open it in order to ascertain, if possible, the identity of its owner and notify him or her that it had been found. To the horror of station staff, it was found to contain the torso of a young woman, without head and legs. From the clothing on the torso – the traditional *camiz* (tunic-like chemise) and *shalwar* (loose baggy trousers) – it was considered to be the body of a young Punjabi girl.

Inquiries were made, from which it appeared that the suitcase had been put on the train at Euston by a white-turbaned Punjabi man of middle age, who had been seen carrying it. The case had a distinctive two-coloured stripe around the middle, and the suitcase itself was large and, as the man had been observed carrying it with a certain amount of difficulty, it would seem to have been heavy.

A few days later another identical suitcase was found abandoned in Ilford, Essex. It lay in shallow water in the River Roding where it flows under the bridge beneath the Romford road. This case was found to contain the legs of a young Asian woman, and the pathologist who had examined the remains found at Wolverhampton was quickly able to match the legs to the body. It was the same girl. Now all that had to be done was to find the head ....

Police hoping to find the head and identify the victim searched the railway line between Euston and Wolverhampton, but without result. It was to be a month later before the head was found. A man was cycling home from work on 8 May near Wanstead Flats. Spotting a duffel bag which lay by the roadside, he decided to investigate. It appeared to be in too good a condition to have been merely discarded, so he decided to open it. Perhaps it had fallen from someone's car or motor bike, or even from a bicycle. It might contain the owner's name and address, and he would be able to return it. To his horror, the bag contained a human head wrapped in plastic, bearing horrendous injuries to the top and back of the skull, the young girl's long black hair being matted with blood. Recoiling in disbelief, he dropped the bag and jumped on his bike, making a mental note of the location, to race to the nearest telephone kiosk to call the police.

The pathologist fitted the head to the two-part body he had at the mortuary, and painstaking police inquiries were put in motion. The victim was identified fairly quickly as Sarabjit Kaur, a teenage Punjabi girl, who was five months pregnant. She had been missing for several weeks, and her last-known address was in lodgings in Ilford. She was the eldest daughter of Suchnam Singh Sadhu, a Barking businessman.

In February she had left the family home following an argument about her father's proposed arranged marriage for her, which she was unwilling to enter into. She was pursuing an affair with a young married man. Her father had ordered her to stop seeing him, upon which Sarabjit threatened to commit suicide. She also told her father that she was pregnant, and that she was intending to leave home to go and live with her lover, who was separated from his wife.

Suchnam Singh Sadhu was eventually apprehended, and immediately confessed to killing his daughter. There had been a heated argument, he said, in which he pointed out what disgrace her liaison and consequent pregnancy would bring upon the family. He felled her with two blows of a coal-hammer and then dismembered her body on a large plastic sheet, from which he drained the blood into the bath. He then packed the remains into the two suitcases and the duffel bag for disposal. The first suitcase he popped into an empty railway carriage but did not actually travel on the train, and the second one he dropped into the River Roding from the bridge in Ilford. The duffel bag he threw from his car in Wanstead.

Suchnam Singh Sadhu was convicted of murder and sentenced to life imprisonment. At his trial, he told an incredible court that he had killed his daughter as a matter of family honour. One is led inevitably to wonder what kind of family honour is felt by the rest of his family whose paterfamilias is serving life in prison for murder.

19

The Map-reading Madman

The multiple murderer who is the subject of this chapter was probably unique in that he planned his killings carefully with the aid of maps, on which he marked remote areas which he had first checked out during the course of travelling literally thousands of miles in his car to find them. When eventually he was arrested, quantities of maps were discovered in both his home and his car, covering the states of Washington, Kansas, Wisconsin, Oregon, Minnesota and other adjoining states, and even of southern Canada. On these maps were more than 180 red circles, each denoting a suitably remote area, accessible by a lonely side-road, where a victim could be lured or forcibly abducted. Fortunately the police caught up with him before he was able to claim a potential 180 victims ....

Harvey Louis Carignan was no stranger to prison. When he was arrested at the age of forty-seven in Minneapolis in September 1974 for his string of rapes and rape-murders, he had a record which showed that he had spent more than half his life behind bars. From juvenile delinquency he had graduated to burglary and other theft-related offences, and finally to abduction, rape and murder.

While serving in the US Army based at Anchorage, Alaska, he had narrowly escaped execution following a conviction for murder as far back as 1949. He admitted rape, but denied attempted murder, and was convicted on the basis of a confession which was subsequently challenged in the US Supreme Court. The death sentence was commuted to fifteen years' imprisonment. He was released on parole in 1960.

Carignan had been at liberty for only four months before picking up two burglary convictions, first in Duluth, Minnesota and then in Seattle, Washington. His propensity for travelling around various states was already in evidence, and it is said that while in prison he studied map-reading and cartography as well as sociology, psychology and journalism. He had an above-average intelligence and could quite easily have used these acquired skills to advantage and put them to good use.

In 1969 Carignan married his first wife, but they were soon divorced, and in 1972 he remarried. This second marriage lasted little longer than the first, as his wife found his behaviour intolerable. He would fly into frequent violent rages, and would spend long periods away from home, during which he drove many thousands of miles in his car, sometimes even crossing the US border into Canada.

In 1973 Harvey Carignan met a man who was so desperate for money to pay his debts that he was willing to sell his petrol and service depot for a mere fraction of its value. Carignan purchased the business for the proverbial song, and then decided to advertise for girl assistants by placing want-ads in the *Seattle Times*. This ploy attracted fifteen-year-old Kathy Miller, a student, who applied for the advertised part-time job. On 1 May 1973 Kathy went to be interviewed and was never seen again alive. A few days later her school-books were found twenty-six miles away in a car-park at Everett, but Kathy remained missing.

During the course of police investigations Carignan was questioned, as being the last-known person to have seen her alive. He readily admitted setting up the appointment to interview Kathy for the job, which was proved by correspondence, but he maintained that she had never turned up. Several weeks later, Kathy's decomposed body was found in a field near Everett by a man out walking his dog. She was identified from her clothing and dental records. Kathy had been savagely raped and strangled.

The police were unable to prove any responsibility on the part of Carignan for the murder of Kathy Miller, but in response to the pressure of their repeated questioning, which he saw as harassment, he sold the petrol and service depot and moved first to Denver, Colorado and then to Minneapolis, where he met a blonde teenager named Eileen Hunley, who disappeared from her home in August 1974. She has never been found since, either alive or dead.

In the months that followed, several co-eds (American college girls) living in the Minneapolis area were unfortunate enough to hitch lifts with the balding middle-aged man who was cruising around in his battered old Buick looking for young girls who were gullible enough to get into his car.

The pattern which emerged was of young girls being picked up, getting into his car willingly enough, and the driver starting off in the direction in which they wanted to go. Then he would turn off on to a side road and drive to a remote area. The girls were then ordered out of the car at knifepoint, assaulted, raped and viciously attacked. Four girls who had been dealt severe blows to the head with a hammer survived to relate their experiences. 'He looked harmless enough,' said one. 'He was old enough to be my father,' commented another. And a third said, 'I thought he looked as if I could trust him' ....

On 24 September 1974 two alert Minneapolis police officers spotted a man who fitted the girls' description of their attacker, and arrested him as he was about to enter his car. A description of the car was also in police hands and matched the car the man was about to get into.

In court, Harvey Carignan pleaded his innocence, and when the four girls above referred to all identified him as their attacker, he said it was a case of mistaken identity. 'Plenty of other guys look like me,' he said.

What clinched the case for the police, however, was the forensic evidence, as so often happens in cases of this kind. The tyres on Carignan's car had a distinctive and fairly uncommon pattern of tread. The car was an old one and that particular tread pattern was more or less discontinued. This tread pattern exactly matched the marks left by car tyres besides the corpse of a young woman which had been found in a cornfield some forty miles outside the city a few weeks previously.

It was at this point that Harvey Carignan's extensive 'map library' came to light. Many of the 181 red circles that had been marked on the maps exactly coincided with the locations of known rapes and assaults on young women. The body of Kathy Miller, who had answered Carignan's want-ad in 1973, had been found at one of these marked locations, and all four of the girls referred to earlier had also been attacked in red-circled areas.

In February 1975 Harvey Carignan was tried for the attempted murder of a girl he had assaulted and left for dead in a field just outside Minneapolis. Still partially paralysed from her injuries, the girl gave damning evidence against him. Carignan testified in his own behalf, and when asked why he had stopped to pick up the girl, he replied, 'God told me to.' He said that he talked to God quite frequently, and that God had told him to kill and humiliate women. Referring to the girl he had attempted to murder, the subject of the charge he was facing, he said, 'I was sorry I did not kill her, because I was supposed to.'

A psychiatrist for the defence testified that Carignan was a mentally sick man, who believed he was an ambassador of God with a mission to kill young women. Another psychiatrist, this time for the prosecution, diagnosed him as a paranoid schizophrenic, but did not agree that he lacked control over his actions. The jury found him guilty of aggravated sodomy and attempted murder.

This trial was not to be his last, however; further trials ensued in respect of other victims, and Carignan was arraigned on several charges of sexual assault and on two charges of murder. He was found guilty on all counts, and his accumulated sentences added together totalled more than a hundred years plus life – which in effect ensured that he would never be eligible for parole.

One Minneapolis resident, a father of two teenage daughters, is reported to have commented, after the trial: 'If that guy were ever given parole, I'd emigrate with my family.'

20

The Workshop of Death

Our story opens on 26 January 1968 in Portland, Oregon, when an attractive young divorcee named Linda Slawson was pursuing her occupation of visiting homes in the more prosperous districts of the city selling encyclopaedia subscriptions door-to-door. At one of the homes the door was opened by one Jerry Brudos, who gave her a warm welcome and told her that he was indeed very interested in buying a set of encyclopaedias. 'They will come in useful when the children grow up,' he said. 'But I'll have to ask you to come into my workshop to discuss the matter as I've got company in the house just now. I suppose you've got samples with you so I can see if they're the kind I'm thinking of?'

The unsuspecting Linda followed Brudos into the workshop, whereupon he asked her to lay out the encyclopaedia samples on a table. As Linda, still unsuspecting, turned her back on the personable father-of-two, he clubbed her to death with a crowbar, killing her instantly. For the next hour and a half he performed various sexual perversions upon her dead body, while all the time his mother, upstairs, was babysitting his two small children, oblivious of what was happening in the converted garage which formed the workshop. As she was to say later, 'I never heard a thing.'

Finally, he cut off the girl's right foot, complete with shoe and stocking-foot, wrapped it and put it into the deep-freeze. He then burned her clothes and the books and order pad she had brought with her in the boiler. Later, in the dead of night, he put the body into his car and drove out to St John's Bridge, in Portland, from which he tipped his victim's corpse into the Willamette River. He then returned home, cracked open a can of beer and watched television with his mother before she left to drive home, behaving as if nothing had happened. Linda Slawson, a popular girl with a close family and many friends, was quickly reported missing, becoming yet another police statistic.

The police had absolutely no clues to go on; the girl had simply vanished without trace. The firm for which she worked had no idea of the precise location where she had been soliciting subscriptions, since she worked on commission and was therefore allowed to choose her own area. The only stipulation was that representatives should avoid accepting subscriptions from the unemployed or from homes in underprivileged areas where it would be imprudent to allow credit, since some of the subscriptions were in the order of 200 dollars or more. So all the firm could tell the police was that Linda would have been working in one of the more prosperous districts of Portland. No one remembered seeing her on the date in question; she seemed to have just dropped out of sight.

The whereabouts of Linda Slawson were still unknown when, on 6 November 1968 Jan Witney, an eighteen-year-old student, vanished without trace, although her empty car was found in the college parking lot. No one had seen her, and she had not turned up for classes. Police spared no effort to try to locate her, because she was not the kind of girl who would drop out of college, or run off with a boyfriend, or even take a holiday without telling her family where she was going, even though she did not live with them. The year drifted to a close without a single lead surfacing, although the police were already beginning to link the disappearance with the case of Linda Slawson, since the pattern seemed somewhat similar: a young, attractive girl disappears without trace in broad daylight in Portland for no reason, a girl with no problems either in her work or personal relationships.

On 27 March 1969 another college freshman, eighteen-year-old Karen Sprinker, failed to turn up for a lunch appointment with her mother. Karen was yet another reliable girl who, if she had been unable for any reason to keep the appointment, would have telephoned home to let her mother know; if she had been taken ill, she would have asked a fellow-student to call her mother. Later it was discovered that she had never arrived for the morning's classes.

On 27 April 1969, Linda Salee, a twenty-two-year-old office

worker, failed to keep a date with her boyfriend. He said that she had never before 'stood him up' and that on the one occasion in the eighteen months of their friendship when she could not keep a date she had telephoned him at his office to let him know. He called Linda's parents to find out whether they knew anything, and they told him that they had seen her the same day and that she had told them she was going to meet him. They decided to report her missing. Like Karen Sprinker, she had just simply vanished off the street in broad daylight, and like Karen she had joined the growing list of missing person reports the police were fruitlessly puzzling over.

On 10 May a man fishing in the Long Tom River, a tributary of the Willamette River, hooked the naked body of Linda Salee. She had been savagely raped, strangled, and her body weighted with part of a car's transmission. Two days later, another girl's body was discovered in the Long Tom River, about fifty feet further upstream from the first one, by a man walking his dog. This was Karen Sprinker, who had met a fate similar to that of Linda Salee. In addition, her body had been sexually mutilated.

Police centred their inquiries on Oregon State University, and among the many co-eds interviewed, one spoke of a tall, stockily-built, freckle-faced fellow, who had frequently been observed hanging around the campus on the lookout for girls by themselves whom he could chat up for a date. This description, especially the mention of freckles, matched the description which had been given to the police on 22 April by a fifteen-year-old high school girl who had been raped. The university co-eds were asked to get in touch with the police immediately if they happened to see the freckle-faced man again. Meanwhile they were told to avoid going out unaccompanied, even in daylight – since this man had, so far as was known at any rate, struck only during the hours of daylight. They should not assume, the police warned them, that he would never strike at night – so they should be accompanied if they went out after dark also. If there was no male escort handy, they should go out only in groups of two, three or more. Safety in numbers was the key.

A call came in on 25 May reporting that the man was hanging around in the campus grounds and had already asked several of the co-eds for a date, which they had politely refused. The caller was told to keep him talking and the police would arrive in a few minutes to pick him up. The girl who had called, Donna Mae Hoffmann, was a shapely blonde, and had no difficulty at all in catching the freckle-faced man's eye as she strolled casually across the campus. She managed to stall him until a squad car with four police officers roared up and grabbed him in mid-sentence. Now the university students could breathe freely once more – or could they?

The twenty-eight-year-old freckle-faced man was Jerry Brudos, who was questioned relentlessly by four detectives, but there was insufficient evidence on which to detain him, and they had to let him go. They had looked for some loophole in the legal procedure to keep him, but found none. Doubtless not a few law enforcement officers were swearing as they saw Jerry Brudos walk free!

The moment he was free, Jerry Brudos promptly disappeared with his family to a remote part of the state, but alert police tailed him, traced his hideout, and he was arrested. This time, during the second round of interrogation, Brudos made a full confession. A bizarre story of sexual perversion, rape, mutilation and murder poured from his lips. He even admitted to necrophilia. A search warrant was obtained for his home, and a box containing forty pairs of women's shoes was found hidden in the attic – Brudos was a self-confessed shoe and foot fetishist.

But it was the garage, a building separate from the house, which proved to have been his workshop of death and the centre of his nefarious activities. He had converted the garage into a veritable charnel-house. There was a large iron hook in the ceiling, from which he suspended the bodies of his victims when he abused them after death. He also had a vast collection of undergarments in which he dressed his victims' dead bodies before photographing them. Albums of glossy prints provided ample evidence of the horrendous activities he had perpetrated in the privacy of his workshop.

On 27 June 1969 Jerry Brudos pleaded guilty to murder, dropping an earlier plea of not guilty to murder by reason of insanity. Seven doctors had found him sane, despite his having been diagnosed as having a personality disorder, but this, they averred, did not constitute legal insanity. It was revealed that he had had psychiatric counselling at the age of seventeen, and that subsequently he had been discharged from the US army after only eight months' service because of the obsessions which dominated his life.

All his life Jerry Brudos had been repressed by his mother, which eventually developed into an overt hatred and no doubt played a significant part in his campaign of death against women. His ex-wife stated that, although he had made perverted sexual demands upon her, he had not ill-treated her otherwise, and he had been a good father to their two children. She had recognized that he had some kind of mental disturbance, and spoke of the severe migraines from which he had suffered, which were always followed by bouts of odd behaviour. She also told how he would lock himself in the garage for hours on end, frequently not even coming out for meals.

Jerry Brudos was sentenced to three consecutive terms of life imprisonment. His defence counsel strove valiantly to get him sent to a mental institution, but to no avail. This gives one pause for thought: if Jerry Brudos's actions do not constitute legal insanity, then what does?

21

Berserk

This chapter is not for the squeamish. It describes how Dale Merle Nelson, a thirty-one-year-old logger, came to perpetrate the ghastly deeds which would assure him of a place in history as the most heinous killer in the annals of Canadian crime.

At 9.30 on the morning of Friday, 4 September 1970, Cecil Willford, who operated the ferry between Creston and West Creston on opposite sides of the Kootenay River in British Columbia, saw a blue Chevrolet approaching from the Creston side, so he lowered the guard chain on the deserted ferry deck and signalled to the car to drive on. Willford recognized the driver as Dale Nelson, one of his neighbours. Nelson did not speak during the entire crossing, and after a curt nod of thanks drove off on the other side. Uh-huh, Willford thought to himself, I see you're in one of your bad moods. Have it your own way ....

Dale often had what he called his 'black moods'. That morning he had risen before dawn without waking his wife Annette and their three small children and left their tiny frame-house without making any noise. Dale was subject to periodic bouts of deep depression which he found himself able to relieve only by drinking in the company of other boozers in Creston's beer parlours. The feelings of rejection and even persecution he had experienced during his boyhood in Saskatchewan had become even more pronounced as an adult and sometimes found expression in displays of open hostility and aggression, even towards his friends and his own close relatives. He felt himself to be a failure at his job as a logger, incompetent at handling money and inadequate in his marital and social relationships. Eight months earlier he had bungled an attempt at suicide with a shot-gun. He had been routinely remanded to the Riverview

Mental Hospital in Vancouver, examined by psychiatrists, and released.

Back home in West Creston, Dale continued to display the same pattern of moody unpredictability. To his wife, he was an average husband and good to the children, and helpful around the house, but after a lengthy beer-drinking session he was inclined to be truculent, even violent. Five months after his release from the hospital he appeared in court in Creston charged with assaulting his wife. Judge Harold Langston dealt with the case as a routine domestic quarrel and placed him on probation for a year, adding that Nelson had nothing more than a drink problem.

Dale was looking for work, and hoped to be taken on for the day by one of the local logging contractors. Jobs were hard to find in rural Creston (pop.3000) and timber-men were usually paid on a daily basis. Dale preferred the rugged outdoor life of a logger, which kept his 5ft. 11in. 200-lb. frame in good trim for the long cross-country hunting expeditions during which he enjoyed demonstrating his prowess as one of the best shots in the valley.

Dale was unlucky that morning: there were no vacancies, even with the firms for whom he had worked on previous days. Typically, he was undecided as to what his next move would be, and the old feelings of inadequacy swept over him as he cruised along Creston's main thoroughfare in the old car. Finding that none of the beer parlours had yet opened, he turned round and headed for home. The hunting season was due to start the following morning, and he had to make preparations for an early start to the day. Again he was in no mood for small talk when he drove on to the free ferry on the return journey, and as soon as the chain was lowered he drove off without a word, heading along Corn Creek Road to his own home. That sure is a rum one, Cecil Willford murmured. Then with a shrug he returned to the book he had been reading.

At twelve noon Cecil Willford once more saw the old blue Chevrolet reappear at the West Bank landing-stage. This time Dale appeared to be in a better mood as Willford brought the ferry across from the East Bank. Dale greet Willford as he drove on board; this time he had three passengers: his wife, her sister, and one of his own three children. They were going into Creston for an afternoon shopping trip, during which his wife also intended to keep an appointment with her optician. Trudging around the town's crowded stores was not Dale's idea of how to spend a free afternoon; there was more convivial company to be had in the beer parlours. He told his wife she could have the car for the rest of the afternoon and that he would make his own way home, probably getting a lift from one of his logger friends.

At three o'clock Dale entered Creston's liquor store and purchased a six-pack of beer and a 13oz bottle of vodka. Dale was a regular customer and usually chatted amiably with the proprietor, Joseph Lorenz, but on this occasion Lorenz noted that Dale was very subdued and quickly left the store after paying for his order. Dale then entered a beer parlour which was already crammed with a varied assortment of dedicated topers. He joined one of his logger friends at one of the tables, where the two men chatted over their beer about hunting prospects. The hills behind West Creston are heavily populated with deer and elk, and black bear are sometimes seen in the area. Dale had hunted in the district for more than ten years and was completely familiar with the terrain. He told his friend that he could not stay too long as he had to get back to West Creston to retrieve his rifle from his sister-in-law, to whom he had lent it a couple of weeks earlier, after she had expressed anxiety about prowlers. But the warmth of the beer parlour and the mellowing effect of the beer were already beginning to lift Dale's 'black mood'. However, drinking on an empty stomach did nothing to clear his head, and a loquacious mood was now emerging as a result of his new-found sense of alcoholic euphoria. By the time he had consumed his eighth beer he was feeling quite himself. He went to another table, sat down uninvited and began acquainting the occupants with his reputation as a crack shot. They had heard it all before ....

By 5.30 Nelson was ready to go home, and spotting a friend he went over to him and asked him if he would give him a lift. By now Dale was feeling the ten beers he had consumed, but nevertheless he purchased another six-pack from the bar to add to those he had bought for his hunting trip. As soon as his friend had finished his beer the two men left the premises. As they climbed into Darcy Bolton's car, another friend joined them, and soon the car was speeding along the four-mile stretch of highway that cuts through the flat valley floor. Dale opened one of his six-packs and each of the three men had a beer. Then Bolton turned left, slowed for the cattle grid and cruised along Creston Summit Creek Road, turning right on Corn Creek Road to drop Dale off at his home.

Dale's sister-in-law, Maureen McKay, was sitting in her kitchen chatting over coffee with her aunt, Shirley Wasyk from the house just along the road, when the sound of a car on the dirt road outside the house made the two women look up. The approach of any vehicle around West Creston's more isolated residents usually aroused curiosity, and Maureen was not expecting a caller. Then she spotted the blue Chevrolet outside her front gate and her brother-in-law with alcohol-slowed movements easing himself out of the driving seat. Maureen was quick to note his condition when she opened the door. 'Oh, Dale, you've been drinking again!' she chided him. Dale smiled sheepishly and walked into the kitchen. 'Do you think you could do without my rifle for a few days?' he asked. 'I want to go hunting tomorrow morning.'

Maureen readily agreed, and taking the weapon from a cupboard she handed it to him. It was a 7mm bolt-action rifle manufactured in the Dominican Republic. Dale quickly and expertly unloaded the three slugs that were in the magazine, checked the firing chamber, snapped on the safety catch and placed the rifle on the floor beside him. He left soon after drinking the black coffee that Maureen had given him.

At 6.30 Cecil Willford was just about to close the ferry for the night when yet again he saw Dale's car approaching the landing-stage on the opposite bank, and once more he ferried the Chevrolet across the Kootenay River. He found Dale in a talkative, even jovial mood, on this occasion. He alighted from the parked car and stood at the entrance to Willford's control cabin. Pulling a bottle of vodka from his pocket, he offered Willford a drink, but the ferry operator politely refused. Dale took a swig, returned to his car, and when the ferry reached the East Bank he accelerated up the ramp in a cloud of dust and roared off at speed towards Creston.

Dale's next call was at Brennan's Garage, which he reached at about seven o'clock. Earl Brennan had known Dale for about fifteen years and had even employed him for a short time at one stage. Brennan's business included the garage and gas depot plus a sporting goods shop catering mostly for hunters and fishermen. Dale had picked up much of his knowledge of guns and hunting techniques while working for Brennan. He told Brennan to fill his tank with gas, and after chatting about hunting he said he needed some ammunition and bought a box of twenty 7mm rifle shells. He dropped the box on the passenger seat of his car and drove off.

From another store in Creston he purchased a box of 2.48in. calibre bullets suitable for his rifle, then once again he entered the liquor store and bought more booze, including a 12oz. bottle of brandy. Then he made his way to the bar of the King George Hotel, an establishment noted for the noisy crowd of loggers who favour it for a night's earnest drinking. Dale took a corner table by himself and drank steadily, sinking five beers in succession. He became boisterous, moving between tables and talking with friends, but as the night wore on he told them that he must leave for home and prepare for the early morning start to the hunting.

He now had his own car, which he had picked up after his wife had returned home. It was now 11.30 – far too late for the free ferry. He would have to drive home the long way round across the flatlands. Soon the blue Chevrolet was speeding towards West Creston.

For a man known to be capable of violence after a prolonged drinking bout, his behaviour during the eight hours he had spent in Creston's alehouses had been surprisingly restrained. All the people with whom he had been in contact that afternoon and evening were later to say that he was in a jovial mood right up to the time he left the King George.

He drove the car to West Creston without difficulty along the unlit winding mountain-road between the cattle grid and Corn Creek Road – no mean feat for a motorist even if sober. His inhibitions now released by his massive alcohol intake, a plan formed in his mind. He knew that his sister-in-law, Maureen McKay, would be alone with her small daughter, and he also knew that Alex Wasyk was away for the night at his logging camp with one of his children, leaving his wife, Shirley Mae Wasyk, alone with three of her young daughters ....

Dale Merle Nelson was just nine minutes away from committing the outrage that would plunge the quiet valley of respectable working folk into a furor of horror that the passage of years would never be able to erase from their memory.

Shirley Mae Wasyk had said goodnight to Maureen McKay at about 6.20, shortly after Dale had left her house with his rifle. Shirley walked the short distance along the dirt-road to her own home and prepared supper for her children. Maureen had already put her own small daughter to bed, and settled down to watch TV. She felt somewhat uneasy knowing that she no longer had the protection of the gun, but shrugged off the feeling. Later that evening she telephoned her aunt and the two women chatted for about twenty minutes. This lifeline was a reassuring link between their isolated homes; there was no street lighting in the area. Maureen was therefore pleased to receive a late-night caller in the shape of one of her neighbours, Frank Chauleur, an old family friend of many years' standing. They sat chatting in the kitchen, the coffee-pot on the table between them.

At ten minutes past midnight neither Maureen nor Frank heard the approach of a car until the driver stopped right outside the house, alighted and tried to muffle the sound of the car door being closed, but the muted thud was clearly audible in the stillness of the night. Maureen stopped abruptly in mid-sentence and glanced apprehensively at Frank. As she was to relate later: 'Boy, was I glad there was a man in the house! I felt so much safer ... It could be real spooky out there all by yourself at night.'

Maureen was not expecting anybody, especially at such a late hour. Listening intently, the two friends heard the sound of footsteps on the wooden porch outside the front door. They held their breath as the footsteps continued along the creaking porch and then stopped right outside the door. A tense silence ensued while the visitor seemed to hesitate, as though trying to make up his mind whether or not to knock. Maureen deeply regretted having parted with the gun ....

The anticipated knock never came. Instead, the footsteps receded towards where the nocturnal caller had left his car. Frank decided to go and investigate. As his eyes became accustomed to the dark, he saw a movement on the road.

Walking quickly to the end of the porch, he was just in time to see Dale Nelson's Chevrolet pulling away from the house. Dale gave no indication that he had seen Chauleur, whom he knew, but headed south in the direction of the Wasyk home. Maureen and Frank shrugged off the incident, accepting it as just one more example of Dale's displays of strange behaviour when under the influence of drink. It appeared to them that he had intended to visit Maureen on the assumption that she would be alone in the house with her small daughter, and might welcome a late-night visit from her brother-in-law, especially after she had surrendered the gun. Dale had obviously observed somehow that Frank was there, and quickly revised his intentions.

About five minutes after Dale had driven away, the telephone rang. It was her aunt, Shirley Wasyk, and her voice sounded anxious. Shirley spoke for less than thirty seconds and then hung up; Maureen sensed a note of acute urgency in her voice. Shirley had said that Dale was coming through her front yard carrying a rifle and that he appeared to be drunk. Maureen knew that Dale was a good friend of the Wasyk family and a regular visitor to their home, but she also knew that he was unpredictable after a heavy session in the beer joints. She decided to take no chances, and asked Frank to go to the Wasyk house to check that all was well.

Chauleur left immediately. It was less than 200 yards to the Wasyk home. He could see a light in the house, and as he neared it he saw Dale's 1966 Chevrolet parked by the front fence. Before approaching the front door Frank stopped to listen for any sound, but could not hear anything, nor was there any sign of movement within. Frank knocked; the dim porch light cast an eerie glow through the shadows that lay around the door.

In response to his knock, Shirley opened the door only a little, and as she stood back inside the darkened living-room on to which the door directly opened, Frank was able to see only her silhouette. He asked whether her husband was in, to which she replied, 'Alex isn't home.' As she spoke Frank could see the dim outline of a tall man's figure in the shadows behind her. From the tone of her voice, Frank gained the impression that he was being politely told that he was unwelcome at that particular time. Not wishing to intrude, he said goodnight, and returned to the McKay residence.

Although it was past midnight, twelve-year-old Debbie Wasyk was unable to sleep, and sat in her room drawing. Her mother had already switched off the TV and gone to bed, and her sisters Sharlene, who was eight, and seven-year-old Tracey, were asleep.

As she sat at the little table drawing, Debbie suddenly heard the sound of a car pull up outside. She had not heard the engine – the driver must have been coasting down the hill from the direction of her cousin Maureen's house – but she heard the crunching sound of the car's wheels on the dirt-road as it came to a stop. After some little time Debbie left her room and went to the kitchen, where she saw her mother standing at the kitchen sink, a kimono pulled over her night attire. Seeing Debbie, Mrs Wasyk told her sharply to go back to her room, which she did. She was curious as to who the midnight caller could be. Soon she heard muffled voices, and by moving closer to the wall the child could now recognize the voice of her cousin Dale Nelson. The voices were now raised slightly, and Debbie heard her mother telling Dale to drink some black coffee. Then she heard her mother scream, 'No, Dale – don't!' Silence ensued after that for some time. Debbie, unable to concentrate on her drawing any longer, decided to go and investigate.

Debbie entered the darkened kitchen, closing the door behind her; the only light came from the dim porch light outside, from which a pale glow filtered through the window into the room. The doorway between the kitchen and the living-room was open, but Debbie stayed in the kitchen; some nameless instinct impelled her to hide in the dark space between the refrigerator and the wall. From her hiding-place she saw Dale and her sister Sharlene walk into the kitchen.

Dale looked totally unlike his usual friendly self. He had one hand on Sharlene's shoulder and was pushing her roughly before him. Debbie shrank back into the shadows as they passed her; Dale was glancing around as though looking for something. She then heard him ask her sister to find him a sharp knife. The big fridge cast a deep shadow which hid Debbie completely as she watched silently, frozen in terror, as Dale picked up a long steel-bladed butcher's knife and then left the kitchen, frog-marching Sharlene into the living-room. Debbie crept from her hiding-place without making a sound, and saw that Dale had taken Sharlene into the bedroom at the far end of the house – the room where Tracey slept in her cot. Debbie could not at all understand what her cousin was doing, though she guessed correctly that he must be very drunk. Slipping off her sandals, she tiptoed back across the kitchen and went into her mother's bedroom and locked herself in.

Switching on the light, she stood rooted to the spot with horror. Her mother, her hands tied behind her with a piece of cloth, was lying face down on the bed in a pool of blood. Her kimono had been pulled up above her hips, and for some unaccountable reason the fire extinguisher lay across her back. With great presence of mind, Debbie crossed to the bed and untied her mother's hands; she appeared to be still breathing. She moved the fire extinguisher and turned her mother on to her side and propped up her head with pillows. As she did so she heard a cry and a scream, and gasping sounds coming from Tracey's room. Debbie knew that she had to get out of the house at all costs and raise the alarm. She was too terrified to unlock the door, so she picked up the fire extinguisher and hurled it through the window. As she did so she heard another loud scream, followed by the sound of heavy footsteps coming towards the room in which she had locked herself. With a supreme effort she climbed out on to the window-ledge and dropped to the ground in the garden, and ran as fast as her legs would carry her.

Maureen McKay was still feeling uneasy about the telephone call she had had earlier from her aunt. Frank Chauleur had reassured her that all seemed to be in order when he had called at the Wasyk home, but the incident still bothered her. As they sat chatting, they were suddenly both startled by the sound of thudding feet on the dirt-road outside. Then there came the desperate urgency of the feet crashing along the wooden porch outside, and the sheer panic of fists pounding on the front door.

Chauleur opened the door, and an ashen-faced Debbie Wasyk collapsed into his arms in a trembling, incoherent heap. Maureen tried to question her about what had happened, but Debbie began screaming hysterically. It was obvious that something was gravely wrong at the Wasyk house. Between great rasping sobs, Debbie eventually managed to blurt out that Dale Nelson was drunk and had attacked and beaten her mother and was still in the house with her two younger sisters. Maureen picked up the telephone and called the RCMP (Royal Canadian Mounted Police) detachment at Creston.

Constable Earl Moker's Friday night shift had been relatively uneventful when the call came in. Even the revellers at the beer parlours had managed to get through the evening without resort to anything physical. It was just after 12.30 a.m. when a Mrs Maureen McKay from West Creston informed him in an agitated voice that a woman neighbour had been attacked and that her brother-in-law, Dale Nelson, possibly with a hunting rifle and certainly drunk, was still in the house with two of her neighbour's young children.

Constable Moker despatched Constable Gary McLaughlin to West Creston, while he and Constable Gus Slomba followed close behind in an unmarked car, light flashing and siren screeching. Racing through the deserted town, they sped across the flatlands. McLaughlin was well ahead of the second car when he observed a vehicle approach from the other side of the river. It stopped suddenly, and the driver waved frantically to the speeding police-car, which slowed to a stop. The driver of the other car was Frank Chauleur, with Maureen McKay and her daughter and Debbie Wasyk huddled in the back, Debbie in deep shock. Frank was taking her to hospital in Creston. But McLaughlin was more concerned with apprehending the assailant to prevent anyone else being harmed. He told Chauleur to make a U-turn and follow him back to the Wasyk house, and to remain in his car with his passengers while he investigated. As they parked, McLaughlin was joined almost immediately by Moker and Slomba.

The front yard of the Wasyk house was faintly illuminated by the glow from the porch lamp. Outside its perimeter of light, the blackness of the clumps of trees and shrubbery provided good cover for an armed marksman. A blue Chevrolet was parked alongside the yard fence, but there was no other sign of movement. The house was silent; even the sound of the police siren had failed to rouse the occupants. The officers found a small girl standing just inside the fence – Sharlene Wasyk, clad in only a pyjama top, dazed and shocked. At that time no one knew of the horrendous experiences to which she had been subjected. She became hysterical as one of the constables lifted her over the fence and put her into Frank Chauleur's car. He was then allowed to proceed to the hospital.

McLaughlin and Moker inched their way towards the front steps of the house, covered from the yard by Slomba. They found the front door half-open, and a shaft of light from a rear room illuminated their path. Through the half-open door of the bedroom from which the light came the two officers saw a pair of bare legs. Entering, they found Mrs Wasyk lying dead on the bed where Debbie had left her. She had sustained massive head injuries. Moker checked for signs of life, but there were none. He saw that the window had been shattered.

The two officers then searched the rest of the house. In the far bedroom they found an empty bed against one wall, from which the blankets and the top sheet had been pulled to the floor. Along another wall was a child's cot, and as Constable Moker approached it he recoiled in horror. Tracey Wasyk was lying in the cot drenched in her own blood. She had a nine-inch incision in her abdomen extending from the chest to the vagina, and her internal organs were protruding from the cut. She also had a savage cut across the face running from ear to ear through the mouth. Alongside the body, apparently discarded by the killer, was a bloody carving-knife.

Moker went out to his car to radio for further assistance, and then joined McLaughlin and Slomba in the other car. Remembering that Maureen McKay had expressed fear for the safety of her mother, Mrs Iris Herrick, who was Dale Nelson's mother-in-law, Moker knew that his first priority was to check Dale's own home and then to ensure Mrs Herrick's safety. They evacuated Dale's wife Annette and her three children, then crossed the road to Mrs Herrick's house and stood guard while she and the members of her family left to stay with relatives.

On returning to their car which still remained outside the Wasyk residence, Moker observed a trail of fresh blood leading from the door of the house down the steps, which had not been there fifteen minutes earlier. He also noticed immediately that Nelson's blue car was no longer parked outside. Moker checked Mrs Wasyk's bedroom; her body still lay on the bed. He then checked the child's room where Tracey's mutilated body had been found, but the body had disappeared. The officer followed the blood trail from the room and out of the house down the steps; it led through the front yard to the police car.

Inside the car, the constable found patches of blood on the front seat and smears on the steering wheel. Later it transpired that Nelson had fled the house with Sharlene on hearing the siren that heralded the approach of the police-car. Sharlene had managed to escape, but Nelson remained lurking in the shrubbery while the officers entered the house. Incredibly, he did not shoot at them. When they left to evacuate the Nelson and Herrick homes, Nelson re-entered the house and took Tracey's body. Equally incredibly, in his frenzied haste to make off with the body, he had actually mistaken in his alcohol-hazed brain the unmarked police-car for his own, despite its being of a different make and colour. He discovered his error only when his key did not fit the ignition.

After Constable Moker had radioed in to report two homicides and requested immediate assistance, another officer, Corporal Finch, issued every available man with a rifle and warned them that Nelson was armed and dangerous, but they were instructed not to shoot unless first shot at. Finch then deployed his men at strategic points on all routes out of West Creston.

A resident on Corn Creek Road was very surprised to be awakened at 1 a.m. by the sound of a vehicle outside. Her house was one of the last and most isolated houses on Corn Creek Road. According to the sound of the car, it was moving very fast along the dirt-road and she wondered who could be out so late in the quiet neighbourhood and why the driver should be speeding in the pitch dark. She looked out of the window, but could see nothing; she could only tell from the sound that it was travelling west in the direction of Ray Phipps's house.

Ray Phipps lived in the very last house on Corn Creek

Road – a small wooden cabin in which he lived with his common-law wife Isabelle St Amand and their four children. Paul, ten, Cathy, eight, Brian, seven, were her children from a failed marriage; the youngest, Roy, eighteen months old, was Ray's child. Ray, who at forty-two was fifteen years older than his partner, farmed on a small scale, raising a few head of cattle and poultry and producing hay. The family was very poor – they could not even afford a fridge.

The sound of the car faded into the silence that envelops the hills surrounding Corn Creek Road. Then, suddenly, the awakened resident heard the sound of a shot echoing through the valley, startling flocks of waterfowl from the creeks into the sky, their cries rending the stillness of the small hours. Almost immediately it was followed by a second shot, and then, after a brief pause, by a consecutive series of shots, all in the space of about five minutes. She then heard the sound of the same car once more.

Meanwhile, back at police headquarters, organizing the manhunt for the killer, Corporal Finch was just about to leave and drive to the Wasyk house when the telephone rang. The caller was a frightened woman who spoke in a terrified whisper. She said she was calling from the Phipps house at the end of Corn Creek Road in West Creston. 'There's a man here with a gun!' she blurted. Then she hung up.

Finch was gravely concerned by this latest call; he knew that the armed man must be Nelson. Even more alarming was the ominous silence when he had tried to call her back. He had the impression that the wires had been cut. Instead of going to the Wasyk home, he headed for the Phipps cabin, taking with him Constable Dennis R. Schwartz. Both were armed with rifles. Keenly aware that they were vulnerable to any sniper who might be lying in wait in the bush, they eventually located the isolated cabin, although street names were not marked and signs merely indicated the residents' names.

The house was in a clearing in the bush two miles past the Wasyk residence. On reaching it, the only sign of life Finch could see was two cows staring unblinkingly into their headlights. His partner parked the car at the end of the muddy track leading to the house, climbed out and moved noiselessly towards the cabin.

The front door was wide open, and the two officers

carefully skirted round the shaft of light that fell across the yard. There was no indication of any activity in the house, nor any movement in the shadows around the building. The only sounds were the rustling of leaves in the breeze and the sudden startling cry of a night owl from the surrounding bush.

Finch went in first, signalling to Schwartz to cover him from the shadows. But he discovered he was too late. The body of Ray Phipps lay just inside the doorway, shot through the head. The top of his skull had been blown off. From the position of the body, Finch estimated that he had been shot at point-blank range on opening the front door. Finch stepped over the body and entered the L-shaped room which served as kitchen and living-room. Isabelle St Amand lay beside the cooker, shot through the head; it appeared to Finch that she had been shot from behind as she tried to escape. Once more Finch had to step over the body in order to move further into the room, the far end of which had been curtained off to form a bedroom containing a bed, a two-tier bunk and a child's cot.

Eighteen-month-old Roy Phipps lay dead in the cot, his skull blown apart. From his position, Finch concluded that he must have been sitting up – probably awakened by the noise – and looking straight at his killer. On the bed lay ten-year-old Paul St Amand, the top of his head blown away when a bullet crashed into his skull. Seven-year-old Brian St Amand lay on the top bunk bed; he had met a similar fate. All five persons in the little cabin appeared to have been shot at point-blank range. Five discarded rifle shell casings littered the floor. Each casing lay beside a body, indicating that the killer had operated the bolt action of his rifle before killing each victim.

Finch was badly shaken by the ghastly scene. How could anyone kill a baby? A baby could never testify against him. The man who did this must be not merely drunk – he must be stark raving mad. But Finch's professionalism as a policeman came to the fore as he confirmed first of all that all the victims were dead. Then he looked into the lower of the two bunks; it was empty, and its dishevelled condition pointed to only one chilling conclusion: its occupant had been kidnapped by the intruder. There was no blood on the bed, so it would seem that the child had been taken alive. The frightening thought that had flashed through Finch's mind was confirmed later by neighbours: Cathy St Amand was the only female child in the Phipps household and it was she who had gone missing ....

In just ninety minutes a real live nightmare had erupted in the hills around West Creston. Seven people had died and the killer, armed to the teeth with a high-powered hunting rifle, was at large somewhere in the bush. He had a car, and had taken Tracey Wasyk's mutilated body with him. Now the unthinkable had happened: he had taken an eight-year-old girl as a live hostage ....

At 6 a.m. on Saturday, 5 September 1970, the residents of West Creston awoke to discover that their little community was sealed off from the outside world by a tight cordon of road blocks. No one was allowed to enter or leave the district without a rigorous scrutiny by the RCMP. Every car was stopped and examined inside and out, and every driver and passenger searched, as well as every pedestrian and cyclist. Armed police patrolled the dirt-roads on foot. Even the free ferry had been immobilized; it was as though a lifeline to the outside world had been severed. The old hulk had been towed from the landing-stage on the East Bank to a point half-way across the Kootenay River and anchored in midstream, with her controls securely padlocked. Even if Nelson had attempted to swim the fast-flowing river, the RCMP had ensured that he would never be able to get his car out of West Creston.

When the news of the horrendous slayings filtered through the community, what would have been a carefree Labour Day holiday weekend became a grim nightmare. Fear gripped some; others felt outrage. Some families barricaded themselves in their homes, while others hurriedly left the area to stay with relatives or friends until the berserk madman was apprehended. Sales of rifles and shot-guns boomed, but it was not for the opening of the hunting season that they were being purchased ....

By 2 p.m., although thirteen hours had passed since Dale Nelson had stormed into the Phipps home, there had not been a single sighting of either him or his car. Corporal Finch and other officers searched the heavily-wooded area around the cabin, and about 300 yards from the house, where the road narrowed and the forest became denser, Finch spotted tyre marks and a broken fence at the roadside. The impressions indicated that a vehicle had swerved off the road, hit the fence and then continued on its way. The tracks showed that the driver was heading west in the direction of Ezekiel Creek; while this provided some indication of Nelson's movements during the night, the rugged terrain and the impenetrable nature of the bush seriously impeded the searchers.

When Finch returned to headquarters, arrangements were made to charter a private spotter plane. The pilot was briefed to fly as low as possible over the terrain, with its vast network of logging access roads between Corn Creek and Ezekiel Creek, looking for an abandoned light blue Chevrolet. However, the plane, a Piper Cub, lacked even radio equipment. Swooping low over the groups of officers, it headed towards Corn Creek. From the air the territory looked even more impregnable, the dense forest providing excellent cover for any fugitive.

From Corn Creek the plane veered west towards Ezekiel Creek, and when it reached the East Bank, as the knots of policemen watched it suddenly dived almost to treetop level and began to circle as though looking for a place to land. Officers made their way towards it through the bush as rapidly as the terrain permitted, and they saw the pilot wave and point downwards. He was shouting something, but they could not hear him above the noise of the engine. The men edged towards where the plane was circling and converged on the area where the pilot was pointing. Nelson's blue Chevrolet was stuck in a ditch at the right-hand side of the road facing west away from the Phipps home. It looked as though Nelson had been making a U-turn when the rear wheels had slipped off the narrow road.

Approaching cautiously, the RCMP found that the car was empty. If Nelson had abandoned his car and fled on foot, it would enable dogs to be usefully employed. Tracy Wasyk's body was not in the car. He could have dumped the body anywhere in the area, and the searchers, of course, still had no idea whether Cathy St Amand was alive or dead.

Corporal Marcotte and Constable Rutherford shortly arrived on the scene and began an examination of the car.

They found bloodstains on the front passenger seat, inside the passenger door and on the floor of the car. Two empty rifle shell boxes had been left on the front seat, and a bloodstained hammer lay on the passenger seat; Marcotte found human hairs adhering to it.

Another group of officers began to comb the bush in the immediate vicinity of the car. Staff Sergeant McLeod kept his group small to ensure minimal disturbance to any remaining scent so that dogs could be brought in later. The underbrush close to the car was less dense than elsewhere, and here the officers had much less difficulty in moving over the ground. They walked slowly, examining every square inch for broken twigs, flattened grass, anything that could indicate the direction Nelson had taken in his bid for freedom. McLeod wanted to cover as much ground as possible before dark; the sun was, at 4.30, already beginning to slip behind the distant peaks.

The searchers moved down a low embankment on the right-hand side of the road and fanned out into the bush. In the fading light Constable Laurier Lacoste made a gruesome discovery: a human arm lay in the undergrowth, some forty feet from the abandoned car. It was a child's arm, and its condition indicated that it had been hacked from the torso with a sharp knife such as a hunting-knife. Other officers converged on the spot, and the search was concentrated in the immediate vicinity. The next discovery sickened the hardened officer who made it: the head of a young girl, neatly severed at the neck, lay about twenty feet from the spot where the arm had been found. Further on, about twenty-five feet from the head, two officers found a human leg, and moments later the mutilated torso was discovered lying in the bush just ten feet or so from the car. One arm and one leg were still attached, and knife wounds to the lower part of the torso indicated where the killer had severed the other leg. The body was identified as that of Tracey Wasyk. There had been no attempt to bury or even conceal the dismembered body parts, which had simply been strewn in the undergrowth in a rough semicircle from the car.

When the scene-of-crime team arrived to examine the area, they were able to confirm that the dismemberment had taken place elsewhere. The police were anxious to find out where Nelson had performed his grisly handiwork, since a knowledge of his movements might throw some light on the whereabouts of Cathy St Amand. No further discoveries were made before darkness fell. The team photographed all the body parts *in situ* and they were then packaged in polythene bags and placed in Nelson's car, which was towed to police headquarters in Creston.

The autopsy was carried out by Dr Otto Brych, a hospital pathologist from the nearest large town. He discovered further horrendous injuries. The slashed abdomen and the dismemberment were not the only atrocities to which the child had been subjected. Dr Brych found that her heart was missing, and all her external genitalia had been cut away. The pathologist's revelations posed a hideous question in the minds of the police: since none of the missing organs had been found, what had Nelson done with them? No one actually dared to voice his suspicions ....

On Sunday, 6 September, at first light the RCMP returned to the area in which Tracey Wasyk's remains had been found. Constable Glenn Madsen, an expert dog-handler from the RCMP detachment in North Vancouver, had been flown to Creston and played a key role in the search. Accompanied by his German shepherd Count, Madsen combed the area for several hours, but no trace of Tracey Wasyk's missing organs was ever found ....

Ezekiel Creek was less than 200 yards from the location of the abandoned car. On reaching the creek the searchers split into two groups and examined each side of the road along the west bank. The first discovery was made by a member of the party searching on the south side of the road. He found the leg of a child's pyjamas floating in the creek a short distance from the road. A few yards further on he found a rope which had been attached to two trees. From its position the officers concluded that someone had been tied to the trees during the night. Could it have been Cathy St Amand?

Throughout that day police-cars went from one isolated farm to another, officers questioning residents and checking doors and windows of unoccupied premises. More than thirty-six hours had elapsed since the murders, and Superintendent Stewart knew that hunger would soon force the fugitive out into the open and that he would most likely break into an unoccupied house and steal food. One of these houses was Nelson's own unoccupied home (his wife and children were staying with her grandparents) and Superintendent Stewart himself was leading the squad which was detailed to examine the Nelson residence.

Stewart was accompanied by Staff Sergeant McLeod and Corporal Finch, and they were followed by another car full of armed officers. Corporal Marcotte, one of the officers engaged in this operation, was checking the grounds at the rear of the house when he discovered a trail of fresh footprints which led off into the bush. Tall shrubbery provided him with cover as he followed the trail. About twenty-five yards from the house he spotted a number of broken branches. Moving forward, keeping a very low profile, he suddenly stopped dead in his tracks. The fugitive was lying on the ground, just ten yards in front of him.

Marcotte dropped on all fours behind a thick bush and quickly assessed the situation. Nelson's rifle was propped up against a tree within arm's reach, but the fugitive did not appear to be prepared for a shoot-out. He was lying prone on his back, and appeared to be asleep. There was no sign of Cathy St Amand. Even from that distance, Marcotte could hear the sound of Nelson's heavy breathing. He was as certain as he could be that Nelson was genuinely asleep and not shamming: the sleep of exhaustion after two days and nights in the bush.

Marcotte returned to the road to make contact with the other officers. Superintendent Stewart ordered them to fan out and surround the fugitive, but to keep out of sight, stressing that he did not want any shooting unless Nelson fired first. Soon the bush was bristling with rifles, shot-guns and small arms at the ready; although they wanted to take Nelson alive, no one was prepared to take any chances.

As soon as everyone was in position, Stewart called out to Nelson with a loudhailer. 'Dale Nelson, you are surrounded. Stand up and put your hands in the air.' No response was forthcoming, and the order was repeated, with the same result. The warning was repeated for the third time. Nelson remained silent and did not move. Stewart then decided to send in a team to bring him out. It would be a hazardous operation, and the job of leading it went to Constable Madsen with his dog Count, supported by other members of the team. When they were within a few feet of the still prostrate and motionless suspect, at a signal from Stewart, Madsen rushed forward, loosing Count. The dog sprang forward and pinned Nelson by the chest, preventing him from rising; Madsen then came straight in behind the dog and handcuffed Nelson, who offered no resistance.

Nelson seemed to be dazed and unable to comprehend his situation: Madsen had in fact been fairly sure in his own mind that an exhausted Nelson would surrender without a struggle or a single shot being exchanged.

Nelson stared blankly ahead without a word as Superintendent Stewart and Corporal Finch supported him on either side, and Staff Sergeant McLeod went through the formal arrest procedure, to which Nelson made no reply. Corporal Barr then searched him and removed his cartridge belt with twenty-one rounds of live ammunition and a skinning-knife in a leather sheath. The contents of his pockets included a set of car keys, a one-dollar bill, one dollar in loose coins, and some photographs of his children. His watch was also removed.

The fugitive's food and water supply found nearby would hardly have sustained him during a protracted siege. Barr found nothing more than a half-eaten can of peas and a plastic jug containing less than a pint of water. It was later found that he had taken these from his own home – a daring exploit when the surrounding bush was bristling with police all armed to the teeth. He had taken incredible risks.

The rifle contained one live round in the firing chamber and five rounds in the magazine.

Nelson, pale and unshaven, with unkempt hair and dishevelled clothing, stumbled to the police-car, still supported by Stewart and McLeod. Stewart's first priority was to question Nelson as to the whereabouts of Cathy St Amand, who was still unaccounted for. Sitting on one side of him in the back of the car with McLeod on the other, he asked him: 'Dale, where is Cathy?' Nelson, still breathing heavily, gasped in a strangled voice, 'I'll tell you. Give me a drink of water and a cigarette.' Barr, who was in the driving seat, accompanied by Finch, took the water jug and held it to the suspect's lips, after which Finch lit a cigarette and placed it in the man's mouth.

Nelson drew heavily on the cigarette, slumped back in his seat and said, 'She's by the car.'

Stewart then asked, 'Is she dead?'

'Yes,' Nelson replied. McLeod then asked him how far the body was from the car. Nelson did not reply.

'You know the clearing where the car is?' McLeod persisted.

'Yes,' Nelson said.

'If I draw a map,' McLeod continued, 'can you show me where on the map?'

'Yes,' was the reply. McLeod then drew a rough map on a piece of paper, sketching in details of the Corn Creek logging-road and the place where Nelson's car had been located. Nelson's hand shook as he made a mark on the map with McLeod's pen.

'How far is that from the road?' queried McLeod.

'About thirty yards,' Nelson said.

McLeod and Barr then left the car and instructed other officers to search the bush near the car once more. Again Madsen was the leader, and his dog easily located the area where Tracey Wasyk's remains had been found; the party moved on from there. Although the entire area had already been searched on two separate occasions, Nelson's map location indicated that Cathy St Amand's body was to be found lying somewhere in the same vicinity. Either the previous searchers had missed it, or the body had not been there ten hours earlier. Madsen with his dog progressed through undergrowth already well-trampled by the previous searchers northwards towards Ezekiel Creek.

Cathy St Amand's body was found 160 feet from the road, lying face down in the bush. She was wearing only a T-shirt which had been pulled up around her neck. Her hair was matted with blood, and there was a deep stab wound in her back. Madsen signalled to the other officers, who immediately converged upon the spot and started combing the area for evidence, while Marcotte photographed the body *in situ*. Only after this was the body turned over.

To the officers' horror, the child had suffered a vicious nine inch incision to the abdomen, through which some of her internal organs were protruding. Around the body Constable Rutherford found pieces of broken glass which appeared to have come from a shattered wine bottle, the neck of which was still intact. Rutherford detected bloodstains on these fragments, which he gathered and bagged for forensic examination; the bottle-neck would perhaps produce some fingerprints.

At 5.45 p.m. Nelson arrived at Creston RCMP headquarters and was stripped of all his clothing, which was required by the forensic lab. Wrapped in a blanket, he was escorted to a cell, and within moments of his arrival he was undergoing interrogation. Staff Sergeant McLeod and Corporal Finch entered the cell with a police stenographer and also recorded the entire interview on tape. After the customary caution, the suspect was asked whether he understood the warning, but made no reply. He huddled into the blanket, his eyes staring blankly, his face ashen.

'Do you understand the caution?' McLeod persisted. 'Say yes or no.'

'Yes, I understand it,' Nelson replied.

'Now do you wish to make a statement with regard to the events that have taken place over the last couple of days since Friday?' McLeod continued.

'What's the difference?' Nelson said. 'I mean, it's all over.'

'Did you go to the Wasyk house on Friday night? What did you do there?'

Nelson's breathing became even heavier and he mumbled incoherently to himself before blurting out 'I don't want to think about it ....'

'Did you kill Mrs Wasyk?'

'I don't know. I remember hitting her with the fire extinguisher.'

'Then what did you do?'

'I don't want to talk about it.' Nelson's voice was anguished and practically inaudible. His breathing was still heavy and laboured, almost stertorous.

'Did you kill Tracey? Where did you go from there?'

'Up to the Phipps place.'

'Did you kill the Phipps family?'

'Yes.'

'Did you take one little girl alive with you or did you kill them all there?'

'No. It all happened right there.'

In reply to further questioning, Nelson repeated that he did not want to talk about it.

An RCMP guard was posted in Nelson's cell twenty-four hours a day while he was detained in Creston. He was allowed to see his wife, but had withdrawn into a deep depression and was disinclined to talk to anyone. He paced back and forth in his cell, smoking heavily, between periods of deep, comatose sleep. He spoke occasionally to his guard, then lapsed into a morose silence. To his guard Constable Hayward he said, 'You are all brave men. I could have shot ten of you if I had wanted to.'

Nelson's preliminary court appearance was before Judge Harold Langston on 8 September 1970, when he was charged initially with the murder of Shirley Mae Wasyk. The Creston courtroom, an annex of the RCMP headquarters, was packed to capacity as the accused entered, tightly-wedged between four burly RCMP officers, while other police scanned the assembled spectators for any overt signs of their understandable outrage. A doctor who had examined Nelson said that he was in very deep depression and, in his opinion, mentally ill. Judge Langston ordered a thirty-day remand, during which he would undergo psychiatric evaluation at the Oakalla Correctional Center in Vancouver. He applied for legal aid, and was represented by Michael E. Moran, QC, who, when it became known that he was defending Nelson, received numerous poison-pen letters and threatening telephone calls, but he did not allow these to deter him.

In Oakalla, Nelson was quiet and well-behaved. He was kept in solitary confinement, and spent most of his time writing letters to his family and in private talks with the chaplain. The psychiatrists at the facility who examined him found him deeply depressed and still displaying heavy and laboured breathing which they considered to be a psychosomatic manifestation. Nelson was extremely unwilling to discuss the more horrific aspects of his crimes. Frequently incoherent, his speech was painfully slow and punctuated with long pauses. It was considered that he may well have been seriously mentally ill at the time of his crimes, a diagnosis based on a number of Nelson's own statements. For example, when asked why he had tied Mrs Wasyk's hands behind her back, he replied, 'I had no reason to do it. I had no reason to do anything. It seemed like it wasn't even me. It seemed like I was standing there watching someone else, yet I knew it was me.'

The trial opened on 22 March 1971 in Cranbrook, sixty-seven miles north-west of Creston – a venue chosen because of the open hostility that pervaded the valley. Nelson was charged with eight counts of murder. The judge was Mr Justice Aikins; prosecuting was Mr T.G. Bowen-Colthurst, and Nelson was defended by Mr Moran, with Bruce Josephson as his junior. The jury consisted of eight men and four women, who seemed to be more puzzled than anything else by the realization that this innocuous-looking character was responsible for such heinous deeds. When asked how did he plead, Moran rose to inform the court that his client did not wish to enter any plea. It is difficult to know how the jury may have interpreted this – perhaps as some kind of artful manoeuvre on the part of the defence – but the truth was that Nelson was so appalled by his own actions that he was terrified by the realization that his homicidal compulsions could easily recur.

The Crown was deeply concerned by the case; the sheer depravity of Nelson's conduct might easily prejudice such a conservative jury and persuade them that he had been legally insane. Whatever the outcome of the trial, Nelson knew that he would have to be kept in confinement for the rest of his life, and whether this would be in prison or in a mental institution made little difference – it was still loss of freedom. But he genuinely welcomed this if it would prevent him from ever committing such ghastly deeds again, and it is in the record that he would have pleaded guilty if Moran had not advised him that it was not in his best interests to do so.

As Nelson left the court after the morning session, he had no difficulty in getting through the crowds that jammed the building – they gave him a wide berth, literally leaping aside with shudders of revulsion.

When the court reassembled for the afternoon session, Nelson had changed into a brown corduroy jacket, fawn trousers and a tie – a vast improvement on the rumpled sports jacket and unpressed trousers of his earlier appearance. This seemingly respectable image only added to the jury's puzzlement ....

The prosecutor's opening address not only took him

through the various events outlined earlier in this account, but he was to reveal even more horrendous aspects of Nelson's crimes in the Wasyk house, hitherto not made public. Bowen-Colthurst described how the accused had gone into the room occupied by Sharlene and Tracey, pulled the blankets off Sharlene, who was wearing only a pyjama top, laid his rifle beside the bed and climbed on to the bed with the child, and performed an act of oral sex upon her. The revelation brought an audible gasp from the rows of spectators. But more was yet to follow.

When Sharlene quite naturally refused to kill her sister with the knife, Nelson had choked Tracey unconscious and then cut her abdomen from the sternum to the pubis. Nelson then laid his face in the incision and ate some undigested cereal that was in the stomach. 'The child Sharlene Wasyk, who saw Nelson commit this act,' Bowen-Colthurst continued, 'will in due course be called as a witness for the Crown ....'

The male jurors stared at Nelson with open hostility, while the women's incredulous revulsion was plain to see. Bowen-Colthurst had taken a calculated risk in disclosing Nelson's hideous deeds. He knew he was dealing with an unsophisticated jury, one that could so easily be appalled and outraged that they could ignore the possibility of insanity and insist that Nelson be punished for his crimes. On the other hand, perhaps the more horrendous the admissions the more likely a jury would consider the accused insane ....

Bowen-Colthurst then went on to describe how the police had found the bodies of the Phipps family and how Cathy St Amand was missing. He described how Nelson's car had been found abandoned on the logging-road with Tracey Wasyk's dismembered body nearby, pointing out that the heart and the genitalia had been cut from the torso, and that these parts had never been found. The thoughts of the jurors at this point are better conjectured than described.

The prosecutor's last disclosure before the end of the first day was how the body of Cathy St Amand had later been found in the same general area after the accused had marked its location on a map for the police. He described the frightful injuries the child had sustained: a fractured skull, a stab in the back, and a 9-inch incision in her abdomen from which her internal organs protruded. Two women jurors looked decidedly off-colour at this point; a woman in the public gallery fainted, and two men rushed from the courtroom to be sick. The good people of Cranbrook had to admit that this was just not the kind of thing they were used to.

The judge adjourned until the next day.

The second day was taken up mainly by testimony from police witnesses, followed by the evidence of the nine people who had seen Nelson in Creston on the eve of the murders, including Cecil Willford, Joseph Lorenz, and several loggers with whom Nelson had been drinking in the Kootenay Hotel, all of whom testified that Nelson had appeared to be sober but expressed varying opinions as to his mood. Earl Brennan also testified as to Nelson's purchase of ammunition. Nelson had appeared to be quite normal, Brennan said, but he could smell liquor on his breath.

By the time the court adjourned at 4.30 p.m. the jury had become well-acquainted with Nelson's movements during the ten hours immediately preceding his final visit to the beer parlour at the King George Hotel. The Crown had clearly shown that, at least up to four hours before his rampage of death, the accused had not exhibited any indications of a disordered or diseased mind or mental aberration. What, then, had triggered the lethal chain reaction? Why had Nelson, just four hours later, run amok through two families, killing eight of his neighbours? This was the question that still remained unanswered as the jury filed out at the close of the second day.

By 9 a.m. on the third day of the trial, ninety minutes before the proceedings were due to commence, a large crowd had assembled at the entrance to the public gallery, drawn by the sensational nature of the case, duly reported in the local newspaper.

The third day was taken up by the testimony of Mrs Maureen McKay and Frank Chauleur, but it was the fourth day which provided the most heart-rending spectacle as the two surviving children gave evidence. First was Debbie Wasyk, her long blonde hair cascading over her shoulders as she sat with head bowed, studiously avoiding looking at Nelson. Bowen-Colthurst tried to phrase his questions as gently as he could, but it was obvious to all present that the child found the two-hour testimony of how she had found her mother dead and heard her young sister's dying agonies a traumatic ordeal, and every heart in the courtroom went out to her. After she left the stand she joined her father Alex Wasyk, the only adult survivor of the two devastated families.

Debbie's obvious relief at leaving the stand was, however, short-lived, for when the court reconvened after lunch she had to face more cross-examination, this time by the defence. Moran, perhaps because he may have felt that a 'younger' approach might be more appropriate, left the cross-examination to his junior, Bruce Josephson, who refrained from questioning her on the more gruesome aspects of her testimony. This time when she left the stand to rejoin her father, they left the court together.

Sharlene Wasyk's testimony came next, but certain parts of her evidence were dealt with by means of admission, to avoid the harrowing experience of such a young child being led through them again. These were read out by Bowen-Colthurst and formally entered into the court record, and have already been described earlier in this account. Some members of the jury were looking decidedly uncomfortable as the prosecutor read out the dreadful depositions. They stared fixedly at Bowen-Colthurst in an earnest endeavour to avoid the embarrassing prospect of catching Nelson's eye.

Who knows the jurors' thoughts at this point? There must be very few crimes on record in which an eight-year-old child has been asked to kill her own sister by a knife-wielding psychotic. Were the jurors so angered by the appalling acts to which the children had been subjected that they were bent on revenge? Did they regret that there was no longer any capital punishment in Canada? Or did they have any human compassion for the accused, who was so obviously a mentally-deranged man? By any reasonable yardstick Nelson's behaviour would be accepted as the actions of a man suffering from some grave mental disorder. But the jury had not yet heard the law's definition of legal insanity, nor the views of the psychiatrists who would be reviewing their diagnosis of Nelson's behaviour in the light of these legal standards. As to Nelson himself, it was impossible to fathom his thoughts as he sat slumped in the dock, his eyes closed and his fists clenched as though he were trying to blot out the memory of his horrendous deeds.

The next witness was the resident who had heard the sound

of the fast-moving car at 1 a.m., followed by the series of shots. Then Constable Moker took the stand and described what he had found at the Wasyk home after being alerted by the call from Maureen McKay. His eyewitness account of the horrors he had discovered made a far greater impact on the jury than the depositions which had been previously read out.

Day five opened with the cross-examination of Constable Moker by Moran, confined mainly to the removal by the accused of Tracey Wasyk's body. This was calculated to emphasize the bizarre nature of Nelson's behaviour and thus provide further evidence of his insanity: the sheer lunacy of returning to the scene of crime to steal the mutilated body spoke for itself.

Corporal Finch next took the stand to describe the carnage he had found in the Wasyk and Phipps homes, after which he went on to describe the various searches of the bush with the dogs and spotter plane, ending with the discovery of the abandoned car and the dismembered body of Tracey Wasyk late in the afternoon of 5 September. He then moved on to the capture and surrender of Nelson in the bush behind his own house. His testimony about this dramatic development lasted until the judge ordered an adjournment for lunch.

After lunch Finch resumed his testimony with an account of the events after Nelson had been taken to the RCMP headquarters in Creston. At this point a tape-recording of Nelson's first interrogation by the police was played. Up to this point Nelson had not uttered a single word, so naturally those in court were eager to know what his voice sounded like. The sound of his strangled gasps and laboured breathing, his words barely audible, revealed his voice in the extremity of his anguish. After the end of the seven-minute recording it seemed to the spectators that his agonized breathing still reverberated back to them from the walls. Asked how soon after Nelson's arrival at headquarters the recording had been made, Finch confirmed that it was five to eight minutes, and asked whether there had been any struggle or other strenuous activity to account for his heavy breathing, Finch replied that there had not.

Moran now cross-examined Finch, and again it was clear that the object of Moran's questions was to provide the jury with yet further evidence of Nelson's insanity. Who but an insane man would shoot an eighteen-month-old baby as he sat up in his cot on hearing all the noise?

Now followed some admissions of fact concerned mainly with the numbers of exhibits and the various reports of the pathologist, Dr Otto Brych, on the autopsies of the various victims' bodies. The high point of that day had undoubtedly been the tape-recording of the police interview with Nelson, recorded within minutes of his capture, which actually contained what amounted to an admission of responsibility for the deaths of all eight victims.

One point which, dare I say, may possibly have escaped Moran's notice at the time was that, although he wanted the jury to be aware of Nelson's unnatural breathing and his anguished replies to the police officer's questions, yet Nelson was still capable of recalling his movements in their correct chronological order on the night of the murders ....

The weekend came as a welcome respite from five days of concentrated horror. The early spring sunshine and the beauty of the snow-capped mountain peaks had a tranquillizing effect on those who had been in that courtroom. But while the principals tried, at least temporarily, to push the events of the past week from their minds, there were others who hankered for revenge, many expressing openly their regret that Nelson could not hang, while some openly said that it was a pity they could not take the law into their own hands and mete out to Nelson a fate worse than death ....

Others said very little, but purchased copies of the local newspaper to send to their out-of-town relatives and friends. Local opinion took the view that the jurors would probably avoid bringing in a verdict of insanity simply because it would have the overtones of acquittal.

The morning of the sixth day was taken up with various police testimonies, and in the afternoon the pathologist was recalled, this time to give evidence in connection with his autopsy on the body of Cathy St Amand. To the horror of everyone in court, Dr Brych was able to add yet another item to the horrendous catalogue of the accused's savageries. He testified that he had found the anus of the dead child abnormally dilated, with trauma to the skin around the entrance to the canal. When asked whether this had been caused before or after death, the doctor replied that the absence of bleeding suggested that the child was already dead at the time. Asked whether, in his professional opinion, he could state that the condition he found was consistent with an act of buggery having been performed after death, the doctor replied in the affirmative. Asked what other injuries he had found, he listed a comminuted fracture of the parietal bone and haemorrhage in the sub-arachnoid space between the membranes covering the brain, a stab wound in the back which had penetrated the left lung – a wound six to eight inches deep – and an incision, 9 inches long, extending from the lower end of the sternum to the vagina, from which the bowels were protruding. When asked the cause of death, Dr Brych said that the skull fracture and the stab wound were the two main contributory causes of death, either one of which would have been sufficient to cause death.

As Dr Brych left the stand, the jurors fixed Nelson with hostile stares, making no effort whatsoever to hide their repugnance ....

The last testimonies prior to the closing of the prosecution's case were mainly routine evidence by RCMP officers. Bowen-Colthurst had called a total of twenty-nine witnesses and had entered forty-two exhibits in evidence, and had shown beyond all doubt that Nelson was the man who had killed all eight of the persons named in the indictment.

Moran opened the seventh day of the trial for the defence. He knew he would hardly be espousing a sympathetic cause, and he was faced with the task of trying to convince an appalled jury that the accused's behaviour should, as it were, be excused on the grounds of insanity. 'I shall ask you,' he said, 'as decent men and women, to apply your good reason and common sense to everything you have heard in this court, including the testimony of Dr Halliday, a psychiatrist whom I shall shortly be calling to the stand. He has interviewed the accused and will ... provide you with an analysis of his mind on the night [of the murders].' As he uttered these words, Moran eyed the jurors as though challenging them to define anything unreasonable in his remarks.

Dr Robert Halliday, after being asked to enumerate his long and impressive string of professional qualifications, went on to describe his interviews with Nelson, adding that he had also read the police reports and the reports of other psychiatrists. 'In my opinion,' he stated, 'the accused was suffering from a disease of the mind of such severity and to such an extent that he would be unable to know the nature and quality of his acts or to know that they were wrong.'

'Do you mean morally or legally wrong?' Moran said.

'Both,' the doctor replied firmly.

Asked to elaborate on his reasons for his opinion, the doctor launched into a lengthy discussion of the points which had enabled him to form his own conclusions, the essence of which was that anyone capable of such behaviour must be insane. That much to any reasonable person was apparent, but so far as the law was concerned the sole criterion was whether Dr Halliday's opinions placed Nelson's mental condition within the law's definition of insanity.

The doctor was then cross-examined skilfully by Bowen-Colthurst, who countered every point made by the doctor in an adroit attempt to establish that a sexual pervert of even the most extreme kind is not necessarily insane in law, and the doctor had no choice but to admit that such perversion is not only a monopoly of those who are psychotic or otherwise mentally diseased. Dr Halliday was asked where he would draw the line between such perversions by a person without any disease of the mind and by one who was psychotic or otherwise mentally sick. The doctor calmly gave some masterly replies, although it was obvious that he was, metaphorically speaking, thrashing about to avoid falling into the traps which the wily prosecutor was laying for him. Meanwhile the jurors stared blankly during these exchanges, the medical terminology going right over their heads. It was just as if two skilled professionals were engaged in a private discussion from which the jury had been excluded, and indeed none of the more complex aspects of the doctor's testimony were explained to them. Curiously, Moran sat quietly throughout; not once did he object when the prosecutor pressed the witness on a point he had already answered.

Finally, the prosecutor came to the point where Nelson had fled the Wasyk house on hearing a police siren. This act, he said, indicated that Nelson was capable of appreciating the nature and quality of his acts – in other words, he was sane. But the doctor insisted that such a temporary moment of apparent lucidity was quickly negated by his returning to remove Tracey's body and then going on to commit six more murders. Surely, he said, anyone capable of such incredible behaviour must be insane ... even to the extent of *placing Tracey's body in the police-car in mistake for his own!*

Bowen-Colthurst announced that he had no further questions, and sat down; no one looked more relieved than Dr Halliday, who had spent the entire day under his relentless cross-examination.

The eighth day opened with Bowen-Colthurst calling Dr Roderick Whitman, a psychiatrist from Oakalla, who had examined Nelson six times. Dr Whitman described these several examinations, and gave his opinion that he had found Nelson's thinking logical and coherent, that he gave relevant and appropriate answers to questions, and was oriented with regard to time, place and personality. There was, he continued, no evidence of hallucinations or delusions. He was certainly depressed, but depression is not a disease of the mind. 'I finally came to the conclusion,' he said, 'that at the time of the offences he was not suffering from a disease of the mind.'

Therein lay the doctor's dilemma – he readily agreed, as a physician, that Nelson was mentally ill in a medical sense, but as a witness in a court of law he was obliged to concede that Nelson was sane in a legal sense. For example, the prosecution had earlier mentioned that Nelson had asked Sharlene for a rag to wipe blood from his face and hands after he had killed Tracey; such a request had been made as the result of a thought process and therefore indicated that he was capable of appreciating the nature and quality of his acts.

The judge asked Moran whether, in the interests of giving the accused a fair trial, he wished to call the accused to the stand, although it would be highly unusual at this late stage in the trial, but Moran declined. He would never have risked putting Nelson on the stand – quite apart from the fact that he would certainly be disorientated by Bowen-Colthurst's incisive cross-examination, it would alienate the jury irreversibly. His behaviour sounded dreadful enough as described in the admissions, but to have him relate his deeds at first hand would undoubtedly inspire open hostility among the appalled jurors.

At 3.10 on the afternoon of Thursday, 1 April 1971, the principals indicated that all the evidence had now been put to the jury. After the number of witnesses called by the prosecution, the defence had called only one witness, who had relied largely on the testimony of Crown witnesses to prove that Nelson was a maniac whose bloody deeds could be attributed to legal insanity. Now all that remained before the jury retired was for each counsel to make his final address, followed by the judge's summing-up. The two counsels' opposing speeches revolved almost entirely round this issue of legal insanity.

The tenth and last day was taken up by the judge's masterly, detailed and lengthy summing-up. At 4.35 the jury retired, and the public drifted out of the courtroom, convinced that a verdict that night was most unlikely. After fifteen minutes of deliberations, the jury asked the judge for permission to take a recess for dinner, to which he agreed, excusing them until 7.30. But at 7.20 they returned to the court and retired once more to the jury room. One hour later the foreman knocked on the courtroom door to announce that they had reached their verdict.

Dale Merle Nelson stood in the dock for the last time. He looked straight ahead at the judge, seemingly unaware that most of the public had left.

'Do you find the prisoner at the bar guilty or not guilty?'

'We find him guilty.'

Judge Aikins turned to Nelson. 'Do you have anything to say before I pass sentence?'

'No, Your Worship,' Nelson replied. These were the first and only words he spoke during the entire ten days of the trial.

'I sentence you now to the only penalty the law allows,' said the judge in a firm voice. 'I sentence you to life in prison.'

Dale Nelson walked calmly from the court to begin his sentence. He knew that the very nature of his crimes would render him ineligible for parole. His life sentence would mean exactly that, and he was as much a victim of his own horrendous deeds as the two families had been.